SHAKESPEARE WROTE FOR MONEY

SHAKESPEARE WROTE FOR MONEY

BY
NICK HORNBY

BELIEVER BOOKS

a division of
MCSWEENEY'S

BELIEVER BOOKS
a division of
McSWEENEY'S

849 Valencia Street
San Francisco, CA 94110

Copyright © 2008 Nick Hornby

These pieces appeared between August 2006
and September 2008 in the *Believer* magazine.

www.believermag.com

Cover design by Eliana Stein

Printed in Canada by Westcan Printing Group

ISBN: 978-1-934781-29-6

ALSO BY NICK HORNBY

To Mary Cranitch and Stephen Frears

CONTENTS

INTRODUCTION

by **SARAH VOWELL**

I like liking things. It's just that there are more books to like than anyone can ever read. Which, granted, is an up-town problem, but a problem nonetheless. I'm looking at my teetering to-do stack right now: the new thriller by Irish writer Tana French; *Trying Leviathan,* one of those nineteenth-century legal chronicles that the kids are into these days, about the 1818 trial that decided whether or not whales, taxonomically speaking, are fish; biographies of Will Rogers and Captain Cook; a history of Frank Lloyd Wright's Fallingwater; Richard Price's *Lush Life;* a few petal-thin volumes of poetry because I've been on this kick where, before I face the morning paper's apocalypse roundup,

I read a poem. I had hoped this would make me start each day in awe of humanity. Sometimes it works, but mostly I just read the news imagining melting polar ice caps drowning all the Emily Dickinson paperbacks in the world.

Lurking in the stack are five crumbling old novels by Earl Derr Biggers I scored from used bookstores on the cheap. My whole life I was under the impression that Biggers's tales of the Honolulu police detective Charlie Chan were racist claptrap and thus—hooray—one less thing to read. But then a friend gave me a copy of *The House Without a Key*, the first in the Chan series, and it turned out to be both charming and suspenseful and by the way partially about racism, in that the citizens of prewar Oahu are forced to deal with a kindly, Sherlock-level genius who happens to be Chinese. And so, alas, I am compelled to crack open every one of Biggers's musty art-deco covers with something close to what Galway Kinnell described as "the sadness of joy." (Another byproduct of reading a poem a day is that it leads to the lame habit of quoting poets instead of more morally defensible sources like Human Rights Watch or *Superbad*.)

That to-do pile of mine is what Nick Hornby labels "Books Bought" in his Stuff I've Been Reading column in the *Believer* magazine. The fact that his Books Bought list is so often so different from his Books Read list makes his portrait of a real reader the most accurate I have ever seen. The hope! The guilt! The quest for shelving!

I'm dismayed by how cheered up I was when the September 2006 issue of the *Believer* arrived and under Books Read, Hornby had put down "none." In that column, collected herein, he confesses that he didn't read a book at all because something called "the World Cup" was on TV. I'm not entirely sure what that is, as I do not live in the world; I live in the United States. But from what I can tell, he didn't crack a book because this World Cup thing was as all-consuming a free-time eater-upper as the DVDs of the first three seasons of *Battlestar Galactica* were to me. Not that I'm convinced that this Ukraine v. Tunisia rivalry he describes has the depth of feeling and moral ambiguity so dramatically summoned by the space humans' ongoing war with the Cylons the humans themselves created, but then again what does?

Stuff I've Been Reading is a subset of what Hornby's been doing—traveling, worrying, parenting, getting married, and (spoiler alert) being British. After seeing the German film *The Lives of Others*, he picks up a history of the East German secret police and is intrigued by the "implausibility" of its true anecdotes, thereby identifying the secret of all great nonfiction—that it seems unbelievable. He hears a cover of "Ain't No More Cane" in a bar and reads *Across the Great Divide*, about the Band.

Sometimes he reads books simply because his sister's husband wrote them. "I have the cleverest brother-in-law a man could wish for," he declares, on the subject of Robert Harris's *Imperium*. Lest ye roll your eyes at such nepotism, think back to Harris's *Pompeii*, a thriller whose plot revolves around hoping an engineer can mend the aqueduct in ancient Pompeii on the eve of the famous eruption of Vesuvius. Even though the reader knows full well that the whole town will be buried alive, and therefore who the hell cares if the aqueduct gets fixed or not, Harris is so riveting that the reader can't help but root for the stupid aqueduct to be repaired. I bet every Guy Fawkes Day Hornby's extended family is gathered around the traditional Guy Fawkes Day sugarplum goose curry, or whatever it is the English spend their holiday ha'pennies on these days, and Harris has the whole clan on the edge of its wing-chair seats with yarns about a Russian bike messenger trying to deliver an important package to Czar Nicholas II on firing-squad day. The brain knows the Romanovs will be dead by the time the cyclist shows up and yet the heart still hopes he can patch his flat tire in time.

Mostly Hornby's monthly syllabus progresses from one book

to another. "Reading begets reading," he notes. George Orwell's writing on Henry Miller, for instance, leads Hornby to Miller's *Tropic of Cancer.* Or, more interestingly, nonfiction on the horrific consequences of climate change leads Hornby to fiction set in the future for the simple reassurance that humanity might actually have a future. (Things might be looking up, Emily Dickinson paperbacks.)

With every installment Hornby's *Believer* column about what he's reading or not reading or hopes to someday read wormed its way onto my to-do stack. So it is with the pleasure of displeasure that I report that this collection of Hornby's *Believer* columns is to be the last. He's quitting Stuff I've Been Reading so as to "spend more time with his family." What—they don't let you read books in rehab? Kind of one of those good news/bad news situations: one less thing to read but one less thing to like. ⋆

Sarah Vowell is the author of five books, including Assassination Vacation *and* The Wordy Shipmates.

SHAKESPEARE WROTE FOR MONEY

AUGUST 2006

I t's been an unsettling couple of months. It took me a while to get over the notion that I wanted to go and live in Oxford, Mississippi, after my recent visit there; and I'd only just become resigned to my lot here in north London when Arsenal, my football team, reached what we older fans still refer to as the European Cup Final. I've been watching Arsenal since 1968, and this was the first time they'd even got close, so the anticipation, followed by the crushing disappointment, pretty much destroyed all my appetite for books, if not for words: I probably sucked down a hundred thousand of the little bastards, as long as they formed themselves into previews of the game.

The Oxford thing was pretty serious for a while—although not, of course, as serious as the European Cup Final, which achieved a level of gravity that I have no wish to repeat in the time remaining to me on the planet. Without going into too much detail, after early Arsenal domination, our keeper Jens Lehmann was calamitously sent off for a professional foul on Barcelona's Samuel Eto'o after fifteen minutes or so. Arsenal defended heroically, despite being a man down, and then amazingly and sensationally took the lead through Sol Campbell, who's had a miserable year both on and off the pitch, what with injuries, form, and the breakdown of his relationship with the designer Kelly Hoppen. Anyway, we held the lead for the best part of an hour, and then—after we'd missed good chances to go up 2-0—fifteen minutes from the end we conceded an equalizer, followed shortly afterward by what turned out to be Barca's winner. Like I said, this isn't the time or the place to give you a minute-by-minute account of the game. Suffice it to say that the game was more draining for me than for any of the players, none of whom have been watching Arsenal since 1968.

Sorry. Oxford. My plan was to get myself adopted by the poet Beth Ann Fennelly and her husband, the novelist Tom Franklin. They already have a young daughter, but I can look after myself, pretty much, and I was pretty sure that I could contribute to the household income even after sending money home to my own young family. It didn't happen, in the end—something about some papers that didn't come through, unless Tom and Beth Ann were just trying to let me down gently—but I still couldn't shake the notion that their life in Mississippi was an enviable one. Maybe it would get boring after a while, drinking coffee in the sunshine on the veranda outside Square Books and walking down the road to visit Faulkner's house, but surely not for a year or two?

In an attempt to compensate for the disappointment caused by the bungling bureaucrats, my reading was exclusively Southern for a couple of weeks, and I began with Beth Ann's collection of poems, *Tender Hooks*. I met her and her daughter on the afore-mentioned veranda, admittedly only briefly (Claire will one day find it bewildering to learn that on the basis of these few minutes, I had made concerted attempts to become her extremely big brother), but both of them seemed like the kind of people that one would like to know better. And then, as luck would have it, a few days later I read "Bite Me," the very first poem in the collection, in which Beth Ann describes her daughter's birth:

> And Lord did I push, for three more hours
> I pushed, I pushed so hard I shat,
> Pushed so hard blood vessels burst
> in my neck and in my chest, pushed so hard
> my asshole turned inside-out like a rosebud

So I ended up feeling as though I knew them both better any-way—indeed, I can think of one or two of my stuffier compatri-ots who'd argue that I now know more than I need to know. (Is now the appropriate time, incidentally, to point out the main ad-vantage of adoption?) If I had never met mother or daughter, then these lines would have made me wince, of course, but I doubt if they would have made me blush in quite the same way; maybe one should know poets either extremely well or not at all.

Tom Franklin's novel *Hell at the Breech*—which I haven't yet read—is set in 1890s Alabama, and is by all accounts gratifyingly bloody. So from the outside it looks as though they obey old-school gender rules round at the Fennelly/Franklin place: the man writes about guns and mayhem, the lady writes about babies and home. But as the above excerpt indicates, it's not really like that at all. Yes, *Tender Hooks* is mostly about motherhood, but Fennelly's vision has more in common with Tarantino's than Martha Stewart's. One long, rich poem placed at the center of the collection, "Tell-ing the Gospel Truth," puts the blood and sweat back into the Nativity, before moving on, cleverly and without contrivance, to contemplate the fatuity of poems that use "dinner knives to check for spinach in their teeth." Fennelly's poems aren't mannered, needless to say. They're plain, funny, and raw, and if you want to buy a present that isn't cute or dreamy for a new mother, *Tender Hooks* will hit the spot—and won't stop hitting it even though it's sore.

Larry Brown lived in Oxford before his untimely death in 1994. *On Fire* is a terse, no-bullshit little memoir about his life as a fireman and a hunter and a father and a writer (he did all of those things simultaneously), and though I know next to nothing about the last two occupations... Ah, now, you see, that's precisely it. It's not true that I know next to nothing about the last two occupations, of course. I know a reasonable amount about both of them, and I was making a silly little self-deprecating joke. (There I go again. Was it silly? Was it little? Probably not. It was probably a brilliant and important self-deprecating joke.) But what struck me about Brown's memoir is that, if you have experience of firefighting and hunting, self-deprecation is inappropriate and possibly even obstructive. It's not that Brown is self-aggrandizing in any way. He isn't. But in order to describe simply and clearly how you rescue someone from a burning building, you don't want to waste words on all the throat-clearing and the oh-it-was-nothings that many of us (especially many of us in England) have to go through before we're able to say anything at all. Before I read *On Fire,* I believed that self-deprecation was a matter of taste and personality, but now I can see that it's much more a function of experience—that old joke, the one about having a lot to be modest about, is unavoidable here. There is a very precise description of the self-deprecator and his mindset in *The Sixth Heaven,* the second part of L. P. Hartley's Eustace and Hilda trilogy (about which more later):

> Eustace had no idea in what guise he wanted to appear to his listener—he tried to confine himself to the facts, but the facts must

seem such small beer to her, with her totally different range of experience. He tried to make them sound more impressive than they were; then he was ashamed of himself, and adopted a lighter tone, with an ironical edge to it, as if he well knew that these things were mere nothings, the faintest pattering of rain-drops.... But he thought she did not like this; once or twice she gently queried his estimate of events and pushed him back into the reality of his own feelings.

And that, of course, is the danger of self-deprecation: its avoidance of that reality. Larry Brown can confine himself to the facts, which actually aren't small beer (or certainly don't seem that way to those of us who experience no physical danger in the course of a normal working week); and as a consequence, the truth of any given situation is perhaps a lot easier to reach. Oh, there we are! Thank god! It was actually easier for him than it is for me! He had it cushy, with his diving into burning buildings and his, you know, his heavy equipment!

Still on my Southern kick, I read James Wilcox's gentle, rich, and atmospheric *Modern Baptists,* and *True Adventures with the King of Bluegrass,* Tom Piazza's little book (it was originally a magazine article) about Jimmy Martin, in which the backstage area of the Grand Ole Opry is rather charmingly revealed to be a kind of country music limbo, where Nashville musicians wander around, apparently forever, harmonizing and jamming with anyone they bump into. (The only bum notes are struck by Piazza's hero, who tries to pick a fight with anyone who still speaks to him.)

Baltimore isn't really in the South, I know, but when a new Anne Tyler novel is published, you have to kick whatever habit you've developed and pick it up. And then read it. *Digging to America* is, I think, my favorite of her recent books. It may be disconcerting for those of you reared on Bret Easton Ellis and Irvine Welsh to read a novel whose climactic scene deals with a parent's comical attempts to get her child to give up her pacifiers (or "binkies," as they are known within the family); I can imagine some critics complaining that Tyler ignores "the real world," wherever that might be—especially as Baltimore, where all her novels take place, is also the setting for *The Wire*, HBO's brilliant, violent series about drug dealers, their customers, and the police officers who have to deal with them. The best answer to this actually rather unreflective carping comes from John Updike, in his *New Yorker* review of bad boy Michel Houellebecq's new novel:

> But how honest, really, is a world picture that excludes the pleasures of parenting, the comforts of communal belonging, the exercise of daily curiosity, and the widely met moral responsibility to make the best of each stage of life, including the last?

Nicely put, John. (And if there's more where that came from, maybe it's time to have a go at something longer than a book review.) Neatly, his summary of Houellebecq's omissions serves as a perfect summary of some of the themes in *Digging to America,* although the emphasis on pleasures and comforts can't do justice to Tyler's complications and confusions. Perhaps no single novel can capture the variety of our lives; perhaps even Houellebecq and Anne Tyler between them can't get the job done. Perhaps we need to read a lot.

Ali Smith's brilliant *The Accidental* manages to capture more of our lives, including both the humdrum and the uncomfortable, than any novel has any right to do. The central narrative idea (stranger walks into a family holiday home) is basic, and the book is divided into three parts, "The Beginning," "The Middle," and "The End." And yet *The Accidental* is extremely sophisticated, very wise, wonderfully idiosyncratic, and occasionally very funny. (It says something about Smith's comic powers that she can make you laugh simply by listing the schedule of UK History, a British cable channel.) Here's a little bit from the middle of the book, the section titled "The Middle": "The people on the TV talk endlessly.... They say the word *middle* a lot. Support among the middle class. No middle ground. Now to other news: more unrest in the Middle East. Magnus thinks about Amber's middle..." I should own up here and tell you that *The Accidental* is a literary novel; there's no point trying to hide this fact. But it's literary not because the author is attempting to be boring in the hope of getting on to the shortlist of a literary prize (and here in the U.K., Smith's been on just about every shortlist there is) but because she can't figure out a different way of getting this particular job done, and the novel's experiments, its shifting points of view, and its playfulness with language seem absolutely necessary. I can't think of a single *Believer* reader who wouldn't like this book. And I know you all.

I read *The Shrimp and the Anemone,* the first part of L. P. Hartley's Eustace and Hilda trilogy, bloody ages ago. And then I lost the book, and then I went off on my Southern thing, and then it was way too slow to pick up in a European Cup Final month, and... To get to the point: I've now read *The Sixth Heaven,* the second part, and it was something of a disappointment after the first. *The Shrimp and the Anemone* is an extremely acute book about childhood because, well, it explores the reality of the feelings involved, even though these feelings belong to people not quite into their teens. Hartley (who wrote *The Go-Between* and hung out in country houses with Lady Ottoline Morrell and the like) never patronizes, and the rawness, the fear, and the cruelty of his young central characters chafes against their gentility in a way that stops the novel from being inert. In *The Sixth Heaven,* however, Eustace and Hilda are in their twenties, and inertia has taken hold—there is a lot more hanging out in country houses with posh people than I could stomach. *The Sixth Heaven,* indeed, might have become an Unnamed Literary Novel, as per the diktats of the Polysyllabic Spree, if Hartley didn't write so wonderfully well. I nearly gave up hundreds of times, but just as I was about to do so, along came another brilliant observation. Even so, the third novel, *Eustace and Hilda,* begins with a chapter titled "Lady Nelly Expects a Visitor"; the first sentence reads thus: "Lady Nelly came out from the cool, porphyry-tinted twilight of St Marks into the strong white sunshine of the Piazza." I fear it might be all over for me.

I have just consulted my Amazon Recommends list, just in case anything took my fancy, and the first five books were as follows:

1. *Fidgety Fish* by Ruth Galloway
2. *The Suicidal Mind* by Edwin S. Shneidman
3. *The Very Lazy Ladybird* by Isobel Finn, Jack Tickle (Illustrator)
4. *Clumsy Crab* by Ruth Galloway
5. *No Time to Say Goodbye: Surviving the Suicide of a Loved One* by Carla Fine

It will have to be *The Very Lazy Ladybird,* I think. I haven't got time for books about clumsy crabs in a World Cup month. ✳

SEPTEMBER 2006

You have probably noticed that we don't think much of scientists, here at Believer Towers. The Polysyllabic Spree, the eighty-seven white-robed and intimidatingly effete young men and women who edit this magazine, are convinced that the real work in our society is done by poets, novelists, animators, experimental filmmakers, drone-metal engineers, and the rest of the riffraff who typically populate the pages of this magazine. I, however, am not so sure; which is why, after a great deal of agonized internal debate, I have decided to introduce a Scientist of the Month Award. As will become clear, this month's winner, Matthias Wittlinger of the University of Ulm, in Germany, is a worthy one, but I am very worried about several, if not all, of the months to come. I don't really know much about science, and my fear is that we'll end up giving the prize to the same old faces, month after month after month. A word in Marie Curie's ear: I hope you have plenty of room on your mantelpiece. Without giving anything away, you're going to need it.

According to the June 29 edition of the *Economist,* Matthias Wittlinger decided to investigate a long-held but never proven suspicion that what enables an ant to find his (or her) way home to the nest is a built-in pedometer—in other words, they count their steps. He tested this hypothesis in an ingenious way. First, he made the ants walk through a ten-meter tunnel to get food; he then made them walk back to their nests through a different ten-meter tunnel. But the fun really started once they'd got the hang of this. Wittlinger trimmed the legs of one group of ants, in order to shorten the stride pattern; another group was put on stilts made out of pig bristle, so that their steps became much bigger. The results were satisfying. The ants with little legs stopped about four meters short of the nest; the ants on stilts, meanwhile, overshot by fifteen feet. Anyone who thinks that someone other than Wittlinger is a more deserving recipient of the inaugural Stuff I've Been Reading Scientist of the Month Award is, to put it bluntly, an idiot. Science doesn't get any better than this.

I'm delighted for Matthias, of course, but I am also feeling a little rueful. For many years now, I've been trimming and lengthening ants' legs, mostly because the concentration and discipline involved have allowed me to forgo all sexual activity. (I have been using pieces of old guitar string for the stilts, and guitar string is funnier than pig bristle, because the ants kind of bounce along.) I wasn't, however, doing it in a particularly purposeful way—I had no idea that I could have been written about in the *Economist,* or that I could win prestigious awards. And anyway, I was making an elementary error: I was trimming and lengthening the legs of *the same ants*—and this, I see now, was completely and utterly point-less: three hours of microsurgery on each ant and they all ended up the same height anyway.

Cynics don't read the *Believer,* which is fortunate, because a cynic might say that the introduction of the Scientist of the Month award is a desperate attempt to draw attention away from the stark, sad entry under Books Read at the top of this page. And a clever cynic might wonder whether the absence of read books, and there-fore the appearance of the award, have anything to do with the ar-rival of the World Cup, a football [*sic*] tournament that every four years consumes the inhabitants of every country in the world bar the U.S. The truth is that the World Cup *allowed* me to introduce the award. I'd been meaning to do it for years, but space had always prevented me from doing so. Now that I have no books to write about, I can fulfill what can be described, without exaggeration, as a lifelong dream.

I wish I had read some books this month, to be honest, and not just because I wouldn't have to drivel on about nothing for a cou-ple of pages. It's not that I believe reading is more important than sport, but there have been moments during this last month when I knew, beyond any shadow of a doubt, that I was wasting my time and yet made no effort to turn off the TV and do something more constructive. Watching Ukraine v. Tunisia can in part be explained by my bet on Andrei Shevchenko to score during the game. (He did, after taking a dive to win a penalty that he himself took.) But I have no way of rationalizing my willingness to stick with Ukraine v. Switzerland, even after it was clear that it was going to be perhaps the most pointless and boring ninety minutes in the history of not only soccer but of all human activity. Couldn't I have read some-thing at some point during the second half? A couple of Dylan Thomas's letters, say? They were right there, on the bookshelf be-hind the sofa.

It wasn't a very good World Cup. The star players all underperformed; everybody was too scared of losing; there were too few goals, too many red and yellow cards; and there was way too much cheating and diving and shirt pulling. And yet the rhythm of a World Cup day is unimprovable, if you don't have a proper job. You wake up in the morning, do a little online betting, read the previews of the games in the newspaper, maybe watch the highlights program you recorded the previous night. The first game is at two, so just beforehand you are joined by other friends without proper jobs (some of whom won't leave until eleven that night); it finishes at four, when you repair to the garden, smoke, drink tea, and kick a ball about with any of your children who happen to be there. The second game finishes at seven, just in time for bed, bath, and story time, and I don't know about you, but we used the "live pause" feature on our digital system for the eight o'clock game—there was a heat wave in Europe, and my kids took a while to get to sleep. Food was ordered at halftime and delivered during the second half. Has there ever been a better way to live than this? Friends, football, takeaways, no work… One can only presume that if Robert Owen and those guys had waited a couple of hundred years for the invention of the World Cup, takeaway food, digital TV, and work-shy friends, there was no way any utopian experiment could have failed.

For maybe the first time in my life, however, I have begun to sympathize with Americans who find the game baffling and slow. The lack of goals has never bothered any football [sic] fan, but when it becomes clear that a team doesn't even *want* to score one, that they'd rather take their chances in a penalty shoot-out, then the lack of action ceases to become a matter of taste and starts to look like a fatal flaw in the tournament. If you're so scared of losing, don't enter! Stay home! Let Belgium and Lithuania play instead! Many teams played with one striker, playing all on his own against two or three defenders; England's striker Wayne Rooney became so frustrated by these odds that he attempted to even them out by stamping on the balls of one of the defenders looking after him.

We can be pretty sure that it hurts, having your testicles stamped on, but I understand that Americans have come to refer contemptuously to the more theatrical World Cup injuries as the "flop and bawl"—the implication being, I think, that these players are feigning their distress. First of all, you must understand that the rest of the world is more susceptible to pain than you. Our smoking, our poor diets, and our heightened sensitivities (to both literature and life) mean that even a slight push in the back can send excruciating agony coursing through our bodies. You, however, because of your all-meat diet and your status as a bullying superpower, feel nothing, either emotionally or physically, at any time. So you can sneer at our floppers and bawlers if you want, but what does that say about you? How can you ever understand a novel if you don't understand pain?

And secondly, these players are terrible, awful cheats. It wasn't always like this. But ten or so years ago, those in charge of the game decided, laudably, that they wanted to encourage the more creative players, which meant penalizing the defenders whose job it was to stifle that creativity. Nobody foresaw what would happen as a result: that these creative players would spend more time trying to land their opponents with a yellow or red card than they would trying to score a goal. (A yellow card means that the recipient is frightened of making a tackle for the rest of the game; a red card means he can't take any further part. Either is useful for the opposing team, which means there's too much of an incentive to fake an injury at the moment.) In my book *Fever Pitch,* which was first published in 1992 (and you can take great literature out of the month, but you can't take it out of the man), I wrote that "for a match to be really, truly memorable… you require as many of the following features as possible," and the sixth requirement listed was for a member of the opposition to receive a red card. At that time, I'd maybe seen half a dozen sendings-off in my twenty-five-year life as a fan; in the last five years, I've probably seen five times that many. It's no fun any more, and it kills the game. I withdraw my earlier ruling.

The saddest moment for me in this World Cup was watching Thierry Henry, my role model and hero and the man that both my wife and I wish had fathered our children, clutching his face after receiving a blow on the chest. Et tu, Thierry? Anyway, flopping and bawling now occupies the same position in our sporting culture as steroids do in yours. Crying like a baby is obviously less harmful than performance-enhancing drugs, but it is a lot more annoying to the spectators.

I have always previously referred in these pages to the mother of my children as my "partner"; you may have noticed that she has now been downgraded to "wife," due to our marriage, two days before the World Cup final. This too has resulted in less reading than normal, what with all the suit fitting, seating plans, parties, and the actually rather distressing legal requirements for consummation. I have read a little, of course. I abandoned a sweet-natured but hopelessly overhyped novel halfway through, and I've nearly finished *Imperium,* my brother-in-law's forthcoming novel about Cicero, which I'll puff next month.

I've been buying books, too. At my eldest son's school fair I bought *The Case of Mr. Crump,* yet another Penguin classic I'd never heard of, because on the cover it had a blurb from Sigmund Freud. I bought Elizabeth Kolbert's *Field Notes from a Catastrophe,* about climate change, after reading the brilliant but terrifying series of articles in the *New Yorker* that form the basis for the book. I thought I was buying it because I wanted to be reminded that things like the World Cup and weddings don't really matter. But then I began to remember some of the details of the *New Yorker* pieces, and I changed my mind: if things are as bad as Kolbert suggests, then weddings and the World Cup are the only things that do matter. ✳

OCTOBER 2006

BOOKS READ:
* *Field Notes from a Catastrophe*—Elizabeth Kolbert
* *Imperium*—Robert Harris
* *Jimi Hendrix Turns Eighty*—Tim Sandlin
* *The Zero*—Jess Walter
* *Fun Home*—Alison Bechdel

BOOKS BOUGHT:
* *Winter's Bone*—Daniel Woodrell
* *Will This Do?*—Auberon Waugh
* *Because I Was Flesh*—Edward Dahlberg
* *Clear Water*—Will Ashon
* *My Life with the Hustler*—Jamie Griggs Tevis

"What we need," one of those scary critics who writes for the serious magazines said recently, "is more straight talking about bad books." Well, of course we do. It's hard to think of anything we need more, in fact. Because then, surely, people would stop reading bad books, and writers would stop writing them, and the only books that anyone read or wrote would be the ones that the scary critics in the serious magazines liked, and the world would be a happier place, unless you happen to enjoy reading the books that the scary critics don't like—in which case the world would be an unhappier place for you. Tough.

Weirdly, the scary critic was attempting to review a book she did like at the time, so you might have thought that she could have forgotten about bad books for a moment; these people, however, are so cross about everything that they can't ever forget about bad books, even when they're supposed to be thinking about good ones. They believe that if you stop thinking about bad books even for one second, they'll take over your house, like cockroaches. She got distracted mid-review by the *Believer,* and its decision—which was taken over three years ago—to try and play nice when talking about the arts; some people are beginning to come to terms with it now, not least because they can see that very few pages of the magazine are given over to reviews. (Do we have to do the straight talking even if we're interviewing someone? Wouldn't that be rude? And pointless, given that presumably we'd be interviewing someone whose work we didn't like?)

The scary woman is not a big fan of this column, which is sad, of course, but hardly a surprise. What's more disappointing to me is that she and I go way back, right to the time when we used to bump into each other on the north of England stand-up comedy circuit, and now we seem to have fallen out. People in Bootle still talk about her impression of the Fonz. Why did she want to throw all that merriment away and become a literary editor? To borrow an old line from the late, great Tommy Cooper: we used to laugh when she said she wanted to be a comedian. We're not laughing now.

I am unable, unfortunately, to do any straight talking about the books I've been reading, because they were all great. The one I enjoyed the least was Elizabeth Kolbert's *Field Notes from a Catastrophe,* and that's because she makes a very convincing argument that our planet will soon be uninhabitable. Usually, devastatingly depressing nonfiction gives you some kind of get-out: it couldn't happen here, it won't happen to me, it won't happen again. But this one really doesn't allow for much of that. Kolbert travels to Alaskan villages with permafrost experts to see how the permafrost is melting. (Hey, W. It's called *perma*frost. It's melting. Tell us again why there's nothing to worry about.) She visits Greenland with NASA scientists to watch the ice sheets disintegrating, listens to biologists describe how English butterflies are moving their natural habitats northwards, goes to Holland to look at the amphibious houses being built in preparation for the coming deluge. You couldn't wish for a cleaner or more concise explanation of the science—Kolbert's research is woven into her text like clues in the scariest thriller you'll ever read. There is no real debate about any of this in the scientific community, by the way. Oil companies and other interested parties occasionally try to start a debate by making claims that are clearly and criminally fallacious, on the grounds that we might believe there's an element of doubt, or that the truth lies somewhere in between, but really there's nothing to argue about. Climate change is happening now, and it will be devastating, unless unimaginably enormous steps are taken by everyone, immediately.

There is, I need hardly tell you, very little evidence that anyone in any position of authority in the U.S. is prepared to do what is desperately needed. Senator James Inhofe, the chairman of the Senate Committee on Environment and Public Works, believes that global warming is "the greatest hoax ever perpetrated on the American people"; White House official Philip Cooney "repeatedly edited government reports on climate change in order to make their findings seem less alarming," before quitting his job and going off to work for ExxonMobil.

I don't often have the urge to interview authors of nonfiction, because the book should, and invariably does, answer any questions I might have had on the subject. But I noticed in the author bio on the dust jacket that Elizabeth Kolbert, like me, has three sons. Has she talked to them about this stuff? How does it affect her morale, her ability to provide the kind of positivity and sense of security that children need? The evidence suggests that our children will be living very different, and much less comfortable, lives than our own; they may well decide that there's not much point in having children themselves. You may not want to read a book as lowering as this one, but maybe that's one of the problems anyway, that we don't want to know. If you don't want to know, then you need to take your head out of your ass and read *Field Notes from a Catastrophe*. It's short, and it's rational and calm, and it's terrifying.

I picked up a manuscript of Tim Sandlin's novel *Jimi Hendrix Turns Eighty* just at the right time: not only is it funny, but it imagines a future, because that's where it's set. Sandlin's characters all live or work in Mission Pescadero, a retirement community in California, in the year 2023; almost all the old folk are pot-smoking, sexually incontinent hippies who have been sleeping with each other, and arguing with each other (quite often about the original line-up of Blue Cheer), for decades. The in-house band that plays covers at the Friday night sock hop is called Acid Reflux, which may well be the most perfect fictional band name I've ever come across.

The residents of Mission Pescadero, sick of being tranquillized and denied privileges by the authoritarian staff, stage a revolution and seize control, but *Jimi Hendrix Turns 80* is not the sort of satire that loses its soul in an attempt to crank up the pace; nor does it waste its characters while wrapping up its narrative. And, of course, it would have been unreadable if it had attempted to patronize or poke fun at the old, or the aging process, but it never does that. Sandlin can see that there is a kind of gruesome comedy in what happens to us, but the humor is never mean, and he loves his people too much not to understand that their grief and nostalgia and frustration are real. This clever novel slipped down easily, and provided real refreshment in this vicious, stupefying (and, Elizabeth Kolbert has taught me, probably sinister) London summer.

Imperium is the first novel in my brother-in-law's projected trilogy about Cicero. I wrote about his last novel, *Pompeii,* in this column, and was positive that I'd have been sacked by the time his next one came out, but here we are. I won't say too much about it, other than that I have the cleverest brother-in-law a man could wish for, and that having a clever brother-in-law is enormously and gratifyingly educative. He doesn't need any help from me, anyway.

OK, I will say this: Robert's Cicero is a proper, living, breathing politician, and therefore perhaps the best fictional portrayal of the breed I've come across. Usually, the narrative in novels about politics goes like this: earnest, committed, and naïve young politician is made older and more cynical by the real world. Anyone who was ever at school or college with a politician, however, knows that this narrative only works as metaphor, because people who want to be politicians are never naïve. Those little bastards are sneaky and ambitious even when attempting to be elected as entertainments secretary. (We need our representatives in our respective parliaments, of course we do, but they are the least representative people you could ever come across.) Robert understands this, although he's a former political reporter, so he likes politicians more than I do, and as a result, Cicero is properly complicated: attractive, devious, passionate, ferociously energetic, pragmatic. This, surely, is how he was, and I suspect our own prime minister must have been very similar. Your president, however, is sui generis.

I've been waiting to see how Jess Walter followed up last year's brilliant *Citizen Vince,* although I wish I'd had to wait a little longer—not because I thought his new book needed the extra time and care, but because he's not playing the game. Yes, it's perfectly possible to write a book every year—all you need to do is write five hundred words a day (less than a quarter of the length of this column) for about eight months. This, however, would only leave four months of the year for holidays, watching the World Cup, messing about on the Internet, judging book prizes in exotic locales, and so on. So most authors keep to a much more leisurely schedule of a book every two or three years, while at the same time managing to give the impression to publishers that books are somehow bubbling away inside them, and that any attempt to force the pace of the bubbling process would be disastrous. It's a system that works well, provided that people like Walter don't work too hard. If the various writers' unions had any real teeth, he'd be getting a knock on the door in the middle of the night.

It doesn't help that *The Zero* is a dazzlingly ambitious novel, a sort of *Manchurian Candidate*-style satire of post-9/11 paranoia. Brian Remy is a policeman involved in the clean-up of an enormous structure that has been destroyed in some sort of horrific terrorist attack. To his bewilderment, he's taken off this job and put to work in an undercover counterterrorist organization, a job he never fully understands—partly because the task itself is dizzyingly incomprehensible, and partly because Remy suffers from blackouts, or slippings out of consciousness, which means that he wakes up in the middle of scenes with no real awareness of how he got there, or what he's supposed to be doing.

This condition is a gift, for both writer and reader—we're as compelled and as thrillingly disoriented as he is—but where Walter really scores is in the marriage of form and content. Has there ever been a more confusing time in our recent history? You didn't have to be Brian Remy to feel that life immediately post 9/11 seemed to consist of discrete moments that refused to cohere into an unbroken narrative. And there were (and are still) pretty rich pickings for paranoiacs, too. Remy keeps stumbling into huge aircraft hangars filled with people poring over bits of charred paper, and one recognizes both the otherworldliness and plausibility of these scenes simultaneously. A couple of books ago, Walter was writing (very good) genre thrillers; now there's no telling where he's going to end up.

Last month I read nothing much at all, because of the World Cup, and this month I read a ton of stuff. I am usually able to convince myself that televised sport can provide everything literature offers and more, but my faith in my theory has been shaken a little by this control experiment. Who in the World Cup was offering the sophisticated, acutely observed analysis of the parent-child relation-ship to be found in Alison Bechdel's extraordinary graphic novel *Fun Home,* for example? You could make an argument for Ghana, I suppose, in the earlier rounds, or Italy in the knockout stages. But let's face it, your argument would be gibberish, and whoever you were arguing with would laugh at you.

Fun Home has had an enormous amount of praise ladled on it already, and those of us who love graphic novels will regret slightly the overt literariness of Bechdel's lovely book (there are riffs on Wilde, and *The Portrait of a Lady,* and Joyce)—not because it's un-enjoyable or pretentious or unjustified, but because it is likely to encourage those who were previously dismissive of the form to decide that it is, after all, capable of intelligence. Never mind. We'll ignore them. *Fun Home* is still as good as the very best graphic nov-els, although it's a graphic memoir, rather than a novel, and as such can stand comparison with *The Liars' Club* or *This Boy's Life* or any of the best ones. Bechdel grew up in a fun(eral) home, and had a father who struggled with his homosexuality throughout his life, and despite these singularities, she has written (and drawn) a book whose truth is instantly recognizable to anyone who's ever had a complication in their youth or young adulthood. It's rich, and de-tailed, and clever even without the literary references.

Fun Home is, I think, a great book, yet someone, somewhere, won't like it, and will say so somewhere. If you want to do some "straight talking," do it about the environment, or choose some other subject where there's a demonstrable truth; Elizabeth Kolbert knows that there's enough hot air as it is. ✱

[Here, Nick Hornby takes a refreshing five-month vacation from his column.]

APRIL 2007

One thing I knew for sure before I started Claire Tomalin's biography of Thomas Hardy: I wouldn't be going back to the work. Hardy's prose is best consumed when you're young, and your endless craving for misery is left unsatisfied by a diet of the Smiths and incessant parental misunderstanding. When I was seventeen, the scene in *Jude the Obscure* where Jude's children hang themselves "becos they are meny" provided much-needed confirmation that adult life was going to be thrillingly, unimaginably, deliciously awful. Now that I have too meny children myself, however, the appeal seems to have gone. I'm glad I have read Hardy's novels, and equally glad that I can go through the rest of my life without having to deal with his particular and peculiar gloom ever again.

I suppose there may be one or two people who pick up Tomalin's biography hoping to learn that the author of *Tess of the D'Urbervilles* and *Jude* turned into a cheerful sort of a chap once he'd put away his laptop for the night; these hopes, however, are dashed against the convincing evidence to the contrary. When Hardy's friend Henry Rider Haggard loses his ten-year-old son, Hardy wrote to console him thus: "I think the death of a child is never really to be regretted, when one reflects on what he has escaped." Every cloud, and all that. Those wise words could only have failed to help Haggard if he was completely mired in self-pity.

Hardy died in 1928, and one of the unexpected treats of Tomalin's biography is her depiction of this quintessentially rural Victorian writer living a metropolitan twentieth-century life. It's hard to believe that Hardy went to the cinema to see a film adaptation of one of his own novels, but he did; hard to believe, too, that he attended the wedding of Harold Macmillan, who was Britain's prime minister in the year that the Beatles' first album was released. What happened to Hardy after his death seemed weirdly appropriate: In a gruesome attempt to appease both those who wanted the old boy to stay in Wessex and those who wanted a flashy public funeral in London, Hardy was buried twice. His heart was cut out and buried in the churchyard at Stinsford where he'd always hoped he'd be laid to rest; what was left of him was cremated and placed in Westminster Abbey, where his pallbearers included Prime Minister Stanley Baldwin, A. E. Housman, Rudyard Kipling, George Bernard Shaw, J. M. Barrie, and Edmund Gosse. Hardy was a modern celebrity, but his characters inhabited a brutal, strange, preindustrial England.

Such is Tomalin's skill as a literary critic—and this is a book that restores your faith in literary criticism—that I did end up going back to the work, although it was the poetry, not the novels, that I read. The poems written immediately after the death of Hardy's first wife, Emma, are, as Tomalin points out, quite brilliant in their...

I think they've gone now. They never read on after the first couple of paragraphs, and I know they will approve of the Tomalin book, so I'm pretty sure they will leave me alone for a while, and I can tell you what's been going on here. Older readers of this magazine may recall that I had a regular column here, up until the autumn of 2006; you may have noticed that when I was removed, I was described as being "on sabbatical" or "on holiday," a euphemism, I can now reveal, for "being reeducated," which is itself a euphemism—and here the euphemisms must stop—for "being brainwashed."

The Polysyllabic Spree, the three hundred and sixty-five beautiful, vacant, scary young men and women who edit this magazine, have never really approved of me reading for fun, so after several warnings I was taken by force to the holding cells in the basement of their headquarters in the Appalachian Mountains and force-fed proper literature. It's a horrific place, as you can imagine; everywhere you can hear the screams of people who don't want to read *Gravity's Rainbow* very much because it's too long and too hard, or people who would rather watch *Elf* than that Godard film where people sit in wheelbarrows and read revolutionary poetry out loud. (I saw poor Amy Sedaris down there, by the way. I won't go into what they've done to her. Suffice to say that she won't be making any jokes for a while.)

Luckily, I have seen lots of films where "mad" people (i.e., people whose refusal to conform results in being labeled insane) resist all attempts by the Man to break them, and I have picked up a few tips. For example: I hid under my tongue all the Slovenian experimental novels without vowels they were trying to make me read, and spat them out later. I had a little cache of them hidden beneath my mattress, so if the worse came to the worst I could read them all at once and kill myself. Anyway, if you see me recommend a book that sounds incomprehensible, you'll know they are taking an interest in my activities again.

I have bought a lot of books and read a lot of books in the last few months, so this first postbrainwashing column is more in the nature of a representative selection than an actual diary. And in any case I have been told that there are certain books I have read recently, all novels, that I'm not allowed to talk about here. One beautiful, brilliant novel in particular, a novel that took me bloody ages to read but which repaid my effort many times over, was deemed unacceptable because its author apparently impregnated an important member of the Spree a while back (and some Spree members are more equal than others, obviously), and the Spree regard sex as being obstructive to the consumption of literature. What is the… What is the *point* of having a books column like this if you have to lie about what you've read?

In my tireless and entirely laudable attempts to teach myself more about the past, I have been working methodically through books about individual years, namely James Shapiro's *1599: A Year in the Life of William Shakespeare,* and Jonathan Mahler's *Ladies and Gentlemen, the Bronx Is Burning: 1977, Baseball, Politics, and the Battle for the Soul of a City.* And I read the actual books, too, not just the titles and subtitles. If I read two of these year books a week, then I'm covering a century every year, and a millennium every decade. And how many millennia are worth bothering with, really? I'm pretty excited about this project. By 2017, I should know everything there is to know about everything.

Pedants might argue that there was more to 1599 than Shakespeare, and more to 1977 than Reggie Jackson signing with the Yankees, an event that provides the spine for Jonathan Mahler's book. But this, surely, shows a fundamental lack of faith in the writer. Mahler has had a good look at 1977, and decided it was about Reggie Jackson; if he'd thought there was anything going on in the rest of the world worth writing about, then he would have chosen something else instead.

Ladies and Gentlemen, the Bronx Is Burning is not just about Reggie Jackson, of course. That New York summer there was the blackout that resulted, almost instantaneously, in twelve hours of looting and burning over an area of thirty blocks; there was a colorful mayoral race between Bella Abzug, Abe Beame, Mario Cuomo, and Ed Koch; there was the Son of Sam, and Studio 54, and a World Series for the Yankees. In those few months, New York seemed to contain so much that you can believe, while reading this book, that while Mahler can't cover our planet, he has certainly touched on most of our major themes.

That phrase "the city itself emerges as the book's major character," or variants thereof, is usually the last desperate refuge of the critical scoundrel, but Mahler pretty much pulls off the trick of anthropomorphizing New York, and the face that emerges is almost unrecognizable; certainly there's been some major plastic surgery since the 1970s, and not all of us find the stretched skin and the absence of worry lines in SoHo and the Village attractive. There's no doubt that New York is safer, less broke, and more functional than it was back then. But it's impossible to read about the city that *Ladies and Gentlemen, the Bronx Is Burning* portrays so thrillingly without a little ache for something funkier.

You know I said that you should view with suspicion any book I'm recommending that sounds dull? Well, James Shapiro's *1599* isn't one of them, honestly. It's a brilliant book, riveting, illuminating, and original (by which I mean, of course, that I haven't read much like it, in all my years of devouring Shakespeare biographies), full of stuff with which you want to amaze, enlighten, and educate your friends. 1599 was the year Shakespeare polished off *Henry V,* wrote *As You Like It* and *Julius Caesar,* and drafted *Hamlet.* (I was partly attracted to Shapiro's book because I'd had a similarly productive 2006—although, unlike Shakespeare, I'm more interested in quality than quantity, possibly because I've got one eye on posterity.) Shapiro places these plays in their context while trying to piece together, from all available sources, Shakespeare's movements, anxieties, and interests. Both *Julius Caesar* and *Henry V* are shown to be more about England's conflict with Ireland than we had any hope of understanding without Shapiro's expert illumination; the section on *Hamlet* contains a long, lucid, and unfussy explanation of how Montaigne and his essays resulted in Hamlet's soliloquies. I'd say that *1599* has to be the first port of call now for anyone teaching or studying any of these four plays, but if you're doing neither of those things, it doesn't matter. The only thing you have to care about to love this book is how and why things get written.

The "why" is relatively straightforward: Shakespeare wrote for money. He had a wife, a new theater, and a large theater company to support, and there was a frightening amount of competition from other companies. The "how" is more elusive, although Shapiro does such a wonderful job of accumulating sources and inspirations that you don't really notice the absence of the man himself, who remains something of a mystery.

Claire Tomalin and James Shapiro take different paths to their writers: there is scholarship in Tomalin's book, of course, but she is more interested in the psychology of her subject, and in exercising her acute, sensitive critical skills than she is in history. Both books, though, are exemplary in their ability to deepen one's understanding for and appreciation of the work, in their delight in being able to point out what's going on in the lines on the page. We're lucky to have both of these writers at the top of their game in the here and now.

Robert Altman's *Nashville* is one of my favorite films—or, at least, I think it is. I haven't seen it in a while, and the last time I did, I noticed the *longueurs* more than I ever had before. Maybe the best thing to do with favorite films and books is to leave them be: to achieve such an exalted position means that they entered your life at exactly the right time, in precisely the right place, and those conditions can never be re-created. Sometimes we want to revisit them in order to check whether they were really as good as we remember them being, but this has to be a suspect impulse, because what it presupposes is that we have more reason to trust our critical judgments as we get older, whereas I am beginning to believe that the reverse is true. I was eighteen when I saw *Nashville* for the first time, and I was electrified by its shifts in tone, its sudden bursts of feeling and meaning, its ambition, its occasional obscurity, even its pretensions. I don't think I'd ever seen an art movie before, and I certainly hadn't seen an art movie set in a world I recognized. So I came out of the cinema that night a slightly changed person, suddenly aware that there was a different way of doing things. None of that is going to happen again, but so what? And why mess with a good thing? Favorites should be left where they belong, buried somewhere deep in a past self.

Jan Stuart's *The Nashville Chronicles* is a loving account of the making of the film, and reading it was a good way of engaging with Altman's finest seven hours, or however long the thing was, without having to wreck it by watching it for a fourth or fifth time. And, in any case, *Nashville* is a film that relies on something other than script (which was thrown out of the window before shooting started) and conventional methods of filmmaking for its effects, so a book like this is especially valuable in helping us understand them. There was Altman's apparently haphazard casting—one actor was chosen when he came to another's house to give him guitar lessons, and Shelley Duvall was a student research-scientist before being co-opted into Altman's regular troupe. There was his famous vérité sound, which required the invention of a new recording system, and his reliance on improvisation, and his extraordinary handling of crowd scenes, which required all cast members to improvise at all times, just in case he should pick them out with the camera.... Actually, there's no way this film can be no good. Forget everything I said! Revisit your favorites regularly!

It's nice to be back. ✷

MAY 2007

I have been listening to my iPod on "shuffle" recently, and, like everyone else who does this, I became convinced that my machine was exercising a will of its own. Why did it seem to play Big Star every third song? (All iPod users come to believe that their inanimate MP3 players have recondite but real musical tastes.) And how come, if you shuffle for long enough, the initial letters of the artists picked spell out the names of your children? Confused, as always, by this and most other matters, I remembered that an English magazine had extracted a book about the iPod in which the author had dealt with the very subject of the nonrandom shuffle. The book turned out to be Steven Levy's

The Perfect Thing, a cute (of course) little (naturally) white (what else?) hardback history of the iPod—or at least, that is how it's billed. (The British subtitle of the book is "How the iPod became the defining object of the twenty-first century.") What the book is *actually* about, however—and maybe most books are these days—is my predilection for 1980s synth-pop.

I am not speaking metaphorically here. In an early chapter of the book, Mr. Levy describes, for reasons too complicated to explain, how a fellow writer was caught listening to "a pathetic Pet Shop Boys tune, the sort of thing Nick Hornby would listen to on a bad day." Now, I'm almost certain that this is supposed to be me, even though I don't recognize my own supposed musical tastes. (The Pet Shop Boys are a bit too groovy for my liking, and their songs don't have enough guitar on them.) I am relieved to hear, however, that I have good days and bad days, which at least opens up the possibility that on a good day I might be listening to something a little more au courant—Nirvana, say, or early Britney Spears.

Aren't people *rude?* It's something I don't think one can ever get used to, if you live a semipublic life (and writers, by definition, can never go any more than semipublic because not enough people are interested in what we do). It doesn't happen often—I don't seem to have cropped up in Orwell's essays, for example—but when it does, it's always a shock, seeing yourself in a book, listening to music you don't listen to (not, as Jerry Seinfeld said, that there's anything wrong with the Pet Shop Boys), put there by someone you have never met and who, therefore, knows nothing about you. And what has the band done to deserve this, to borrow one of their song titles? They were mentioned in my newspaper this morning, in a diary piece about their plans for a musical adaptation of Francis Wheen's brilliant biography of Marx; that, like so much they have done, sounds pretty cool to me.

Unnerved, I skipped straight to Levy's chapter about whether the shuffle feature is indeed random. It is, apparently.

The annoying thing about reading is that you can never get the job done. The other day I was in a bookstore flicking through a book called something like *1001 Books You Must Read Before You Die* (and, without naming names, you should be aware that the task set by the title is by definition impossible, because at least four hundred of the books suggested would kill you anyway), but reading begets reading—that's sort of the point of it, surely?—and anybody who never deviates from a set list of books is intellectually dead anyway. Look at the trouble Orwell's essays got me into. First of all there's his long and interesting consideration of Henry Miller's *Tropic of Cancer,* a novel that I must confess I had written off as dated smut; George has persuaded me otherwise, so I bought it. And then, while discussing the Orwell essays with a friend, I was introduced to Norman Lewis's astounding *Naples '44,* a book which, my venerable friend seemed to be suggesting, was at least a match for any of Orwell's nonfiction. (Oh, why be coy? My venerable friend was Stephen Frears, still best known, I like to think, as the director of *High Fidelity,* and an endless source of good book recommendations.)

I think he's right. The trouble with the Orwell essays is that they are mostly of no earthly use to anyone now—and this is perhaps the first book I've read since I started this column that I can't imagine any American of my acquaintance plowing through. If you really feel you need to read several thousand words about English boys' weeklies of the 1930s, then I won't try and stop you, but these pieces are mostly top-drawer journalism—Tom Wolfe, as it were, rather than Montaigne; Orwell is dissecting bodies that actually gave up the ghost eighty-odd years ago. This problem becomes particularly acute when he's dissecting bodies that gave up the ghost ninety or a hundred years ago. "In 1920, when I was about seventeen, I probably knew the whole of [A. E. Housman's] *A Shropshire Lad* by heart. I wonder how much impression *A Shropshire Lad* makes at this moment on a boy of the same age and more or less the same cast of mind? No doubt he has heard of it and even glanced into it; it might strike him as rather cheaply clever—probably that would be about all."

If you try and do Orwell the service of treating him as a contemporary writer, someone whose observations make as much sense to us now as they did in 1940, then that last sentence is merely hilarious—how many bright seventeen-year-old boys do you know who might have glanced into *A Shropshire Lad* and found it "cheaply clever"? So even when Orwell is talking about things that he knows haven't lasted, he is unable to anticipate their complete and utter disappearance from the cultural landscape. How was he to know that the average seventeen-year-old boy is more likely to have sampled his sister's kidney than Housman's poetry? It wasn't his fault. He couldn't see 50 Cent coming.

An essay titled "Bookshop Memories," about Orwell's experiences working in a secondhand bookstore, notes that the three best-selling authors during his stint were Ethel M. Dell, Warwick Deeping, and Jeffery Farnol. "Dell's novels, of course, are read solely by women"—well, we all knew that—"but by women of all kinds and ages and not, as one might expect, merely by wistful spinsters and the fat wives of tobacconists." Ah, those were the days, when popular novelists were able to rely on the fat wives of tobacconists for half their income. Times are much harder (and leaner) now. Many is the time that I've wished I could tell the size-zero wives of tobacconists that I didn't want their rotten money, but I have had to button my lip, regrettably. I have a large family to support.

One of the most bewildering lines comes in "Inside the Whale," the long essay about the state of literature, first published in 1940, that begins with the appreciation of Henry Miller. "To say 'I accept' in an age like our own is to say that you accept concentration-camps, rubber truncheons, Hitler, Stalin, bombs, aeroplanes, tinned food, machine-guns, putsches, purges, slogans, Bedaux belts, gas-masks, submarines, spies, provocateurs, press-censorship, secret prisons, aspirins, Hollywood films, and political murders." Is it possible to accept, say, tinned food, Hollywood films, and aspirin without accepting Stalin and Hitler? I'm afraid I am one of those cowards who would have happily invaded Poland if it meant getting hold of a couple of pills to alleviate a hangover. And what was wrong with tinned food, that all those guys banged on about it so much? (Remember John Betjeman's poem "Slough"? "Come, bombs, and blow to smithereens / Those air-conditioned, bright canteens / Tinned fruit, tinned meat, tinned milk, tinned beans / Tinned minds, tinned breath.") It's true, of course, that fresh fruit is better for you. But one would hope that, with the benefit of hindsight, Orwell, Betjeman, and the rest would concede that Belsen and the purges ranked higher up the list of the mid-twentieth century's horrors than a nice can of peaches. Mind you, when in fifty years' time, students examine the intellectual journalism of the early twenty-first century, they will probably find more about the vileness of bloggers and reality television than they will about the destruction of the planet.

There are some brilliant lines. How about this, from Orwell's essay on Dickens: "What people always demand of a popular novelist is that he shall write the same book over and over again, forgetting that a man who would write the same book twice could not even write it once." There's a great little essay called "Books v. Cigarettes," although some will find his conclusion (books) controversial. And of course his prose is beyond reproach, muscular, readable, accessible.

Naples '44, however, is something else altogether. Norman Lewis, who lived to be ninety-five and who published his last travel book in 2002, was an intelligence officer for the Allies; what he found when he was posted to Naples beggared belief. The Neapolitans were starving—they had eaten all the fish in the aquarium and just about every weed by the roadside. An estimated 42,000 of the city's 150,000 women had turned to prostitution.

And yet there is so much in this short diary other than sheer misery, so many tones and flavors. You might wish to point out that Lewis wasn't one of the starving, and so accessing flavors wasn't a problem for him, but the variety and richness and strangeness of life in what remains one of the maddest and most neurotic cities in the world clearly demanded his attention. This is a long-winded way of saying that this book is, at times, unbearably sad, but it is also very funny and weird, too. There are the doctors who specialize in the surgical restoration of virginity (although before you book your flights, ladies, you should check that they're still working), and there are the biannual liquefactions and solidifications of the blood of saints, the relative speeds of which presage either prosperity or poverty for the city. Vesuvius erupts in the middle of all this; and of course, there's a war going on—a war which is occasionally reminiscent of the one Tobias Wolff described in *In Pharaoh's Army*. It allows for strange, pointless, occasionally idyllic trips out into the countryside, with the enemy all around but invisible.

My favorite character, one who comes to symbolize the logic of Naples, is Lattarullo, one of the four thousand or so lawyers in Naples unable to make a living. Much of his income before the war came from acting as an "uncle from Rome," a job which involved turning up at Neapolitan funerals and acting as a dignified and sober out-of-towner, in direct contrast to the frenzied and grief-stricken native relatives. Paying for an uncle from Rome to turn up showed a touch of class. During the war, however, Lattarullo was denied even this modest supplement because Rome was occupied, and travel was impossible. So even though everyone knew Roman uncles came from Naples, the appearance of a Roman uncle at a Neapolitan funeral before the liberation of Rome would have punctured the illusion, like a boom mic visible in a movie. This is Orwell via Lewis Carroll, and if I read a better couple of hundred pages of nonfiction this year, I'll be a happy man.

If, at the moment, you happen to be looking for a book that

makes you feel good about sex, though, then I should warn you that *Naples '44* isn't the one. There are too many devout Catholic wives selling themselves for a tin of fruit, and way too many sexual diseases. And while William Kennedy's *Ironweed* is beautiful— haunted and haunting, thoughtful and visceral—it too is entirely without aphrodisiacal qualities. The people are too sick, and drunk, and cold, but they try it on anyway, sometimes just so they can get to sleep the night in a deserted car full of other bums. None of this matters so much to me anymore. By the time you read this I will have turned fifty, so I can't reasonably expect very much more in that department anyway. But you—you're young, some of you. I don't want you to feel bad about your bodies. Yes, you will die, and your bodies will decay and rot way before then. But you shouldn't feel bad about that just yet. Actually, on second thought, the truth is that *Ironweed* is exactly the sort of book you should be reading when you're young, and still robust enough to slough it off. And it's a truly terrible book to be reading in the last few months of your forties. Is this really all that's left? ✷

JUNE/JULY 2007

BOOKS BOUGHT:
* *On Chesil Beach*—
  Ian McEwan
* *My Life with Nye*—
  Jennie Lee

BOOKS READ:
* Novel (abandoned)—
  A. Non
* *On Chesil Beach*—
  Ian McEwan
* *In My Father's House*—
  Miranda Seymour
* *The Blind Side*—
  Michael Lewis

This morning, while shaving, I listened to a reading from Anna Politkovskaya's *A Russian Diary* on BBC Radio 4. It was pretty extraordinary—brutal and brave (Politkovskaya, as I'm sure you know, was murdered, presumably because of her determination to bring some of her country's darkest wrongdoings into the light). And its depiction of a country where the state is so brazenly lawless is so bizarre that I couldn't help but think of fiction—specifically, a novel I had just abandoned by a senior, highly regarded literary figure. Politkovskaya's words reminded me that the reason I gave up on the novel was partly because I became frustrated with the deliberate imprecision of its language, its obfuscation, its unwillingness to give up its meaning quickly and easily. This, of course, is precisely what some people prize in a certain kind of fiction, and good luck to them. I can't say that this kind of ambiguity is my favorite thing, and it's certainly not what I look for first in a novel, but I know that I would have missed out on an awful lot of good stuff if I wasn't prepared to tolerate a little incomprehension and attendant exasperation every now and again. In this novel, however, I found myself feeling particularly impatient. "A perfect day begins in death, in the semblance of death, in deep surrender," the novelist (or his omniscient narrator) tells us. Does it? Not for me it doesn't, pal. Unless, of course, death here means "a good night's sleep." Or "a strong cup of coffee." Maybe that's it? "Death" = "a strong cup of coffee" and "the semblance of death" = some kind of coffee substitute, like a Frappuccino? Then why doesn't he say so? There is no mistaking what the word *death* means in Politkovskaya's diaries, and once again I found myself wondering whether the complication of language is in inverse proportion to the size of the subject under discussion. Politkovskaya is writing about the agonies of a nation plagued by corruption, terrorism, and despotism; the highly regarded literary figure is writing about some middle-class people who are bored of their marriage. My case rests.

The highly regarded literary figure recently quoted Irwin Shaw's observation that "the great machines of the world do not run on fidelity," in an attempt to explain his views on matrimony, and though this sounds pretty good when you first hear it, lofty and practical all at the same time, on further reflection it starts to fall apart. If we are going to judge things on their ability to power the great machines of the world, then we will have to agree that music, charity, tolerance, and bacon-flavored potato chips, to name only four things that we prize here at the *Believer,* are worse than useless.

It wasn't just the opacity of the prose that led me to abandon the novel, however; I didn't like the characters who populated it much, either. They were all languidly middle class, and they drank good wine and talked about Sartre, and I didn't want to know anything about them. This is entirely unreasonable of me, I accept that. But prejudice has to be an important part of our decision-making process when it comes to reading; otherwise we would become overwhelmed. For months I have been refusing to read a novel that a couple of friends have been urging upon me, a novel that received wonderful reviews and got nominated for prestigious prizes. I'm sure it's great, but I know it's not for me: the author is posh—posh English, which is somehow worse than posh American, even—and he writes about posh people, and I have taken the view that life is too short to spend any time worrying about the travails of the English upper classes. If you had spent the last half century listening to the strangled vows and the unexamined, usually very dim assumptions that frequently emerge from the mouths of a certain kind of Englishman, you'd feel entitled to a little bit of inverted snobbery.

I'm not sure, then, quite how I was persuaded to read *In My Father's House,* Miranda Seymour's memoir about her extraordinary father and his almost demented devotion to Thrumpton Hall, the stately home he came to inherit. George Seymour was a terrible snob, pathetically obsessed by the microscopic traces of blue blood that ran through his veins, comically observant of every single nonsensical English upper-class propriety—until he reached middle age, when he bought himself a motorbike and drove around England and Europe with a young man called Nick, with whom he shared a bedroom. Nick was replaced by Robbie, whom George called Tigger, after the A. A. Milne character; when Robbie shot himself in the head, a weeping George played the Disney song on a scratchy vinyl record at the funeral service. Actually, you can probably see why I was persuaded to read it: It's a terrific story, and Miranda Seymour is too good a writer not to recognize its peculiarities and its worth. Also, the same people who have been telling me to read the posh novel told me to read the posh memoir, and I felt that a further refusal would have indicated some kind of Trotskyite militancy that I really don't feel. It's more a mild distaste than a deeply entrenched worldview.

Miranda Seymour owns up to having inherited her father's snobbery, which meant that I was immediately put on the alert, ready to abandon the book and condemn the author to the legions of the unnameable, but there is nothing much here to send one to the barricades. There is one strange moment, however, a couple of sentences that I read and re-read in order to check that I wasn't missing the irony. When Seymour goes to visit some of her father's wartime friends to gather their recollections, she finds herself resenting what she perceives as their feelings of superiority; they saw active service and George Seymour didn't, and the daughter is defensive on the father's behalf: "I've plenty of reason to hate my father, but his achievement matches theirs. They've no cause to be disdainful. They fought for their country; he gave his life to save a house."

Where does one begin with this? Perhaps one should simply point out that George died in his bed (a bed within a bedroom within one of Britain's loveliest houses) at the age of seventy-one, so the expression "he gave his life" does not have the conventional meaning here; a more exact rendering would be something like "he put aside an awful lot of time." It's a curious lapse in judgment in an otherwise carefully nuanced book.

A couple of years ago, I wrote in this column about Michael Lewis's brilliant *Moneyball;* when I found during a recent trip to New York that Lewis had written a book about football, I was off to the till before you could say "Jackie Robinson." *The Blind Side* is very nearly as good, I think, which is saying something, seeing as *Moneyball* is one of the two or three best sports books I have ever read. It cleverly combines two stories, one personal, the other an account of the recent history of the game; Lewis explains how left tackle became the most remunerative position in football, then allows the weight of this history to settle on the shoulders of one young man, Michael Oher, currently at Ole Miss (I'm finding my effortless use of the American vernacular strangely thrilling). Oher is six foot six, weighs 330 pounds, and yet he can run hundreds of yards in fractions of seconds. He is, as he keeps being told, a freak of nature, and he is exactly what every football team in the U.S. is prepared to offer the earth for.

He has also had a life well beyond the realms of the ordinary, which makes his story... well, I'm afraid my knowledge of the terminology has already been exhausted, but in my sport we'd describe it as an open goal, and Lewis only has to tap the ball in from a couple of feet. I don't wish to diminish the author's achievement. Lewis scores with his customary brio, and the recognition of a good story is an enviable part of his talent. But who wouldn't want to read about a kid who was born to a crack-addict mother and partially raised in one of the poorest parts of one of America's poorest cities, Memphis, before being adopted by a wealthy white Christian couple with their own private plane? This is material that provides the pleasures of both fiction and nonfiction. There's a compelling narrative arc, a glimpse into the lives of others, a wealth of information about and analysis of a central element of popular American culture. There's a touching central relationship, between Oher and his adoptive parents' young son, Sean Jr.; there is even a cheesy, never-say-die heroine, Oher's adoptive mother, Leigh Anne Tuohy, whose extraordinary determination to look after a boy not her own is Christian in the sense too rarely associated with the American South. It would make a great movie, although you'd need a lot of CGI to convince an audience of Michael Oher's speed and size.

The Blind Side is funny, too. Michael's first game for his high school is made distinctive by his lifting up his two-hundred-and-twenty-pound opponent and taking him through the opposition benches, across the cinder track surrounding the pitch, and halfway across a neighboring field before he is stopped by players and officials from both sides. (Oher had been irritated and surprised by the opponent's trash-talking—he later told his coach he was going to put the lippy kid back on his team bus.) And the formal interview between Oher and an investigator from the NCAA, the organization whose job it is to determine whether any illegal inducements have been offered to influence a promising footballer's choice of college, is equally memorable. It's not just Oher's attempts to list his brothers and sisters that baffle the investigator; it's the opulence of his surroundings, too. The Tuohys are Ole Miss alumni, desperate for Michael to take the scholarship being offered by their alma mater while trying to avoid putting inappropriate pressure on him. But isn't Oher's whole new life—the access to the jet, the new car, the pool, the exclusive private high school—a form of inappropriate pressure? The baffled investigator eventually decides not, but she is clearly perplexed by the atypicality of the arrangement.

Ian McEwan has hit that enviable moment that comes to a novelist only very rarely: he has written himself into a position where everyone wants to read his latest book *now, today,* before any other bastard comes along and ruins it. He's genuinely serious and genuinely popular, in the U.K. at least, and in an age where our tastes in culture are becoming ever more refined, and therefore ever more fractured, he is almost single-handedly reviving the notion of a chattering class by providing something that we can all chatter about. *On Chesil Beach* is, for me, a return to top form after the unevenness of *Saturday.* It's unusual, on occasions painfully real, and ultimately very moving.

Philip Larkin famously wrote that "Sexual intercourse began / In nineteen sixty-three / (Which was rather late for me) / Between the end of the Chatterley ban / And the Beatles' first LP." *On Chesil Beach* is set on a July night in 1962, and sexual intercourse is about to begin for Edward and Florence, married that afternoon and painfully inexperienced. Edward wants it and Florence doesn't, and that, pretty much, is where the drama and the pain of the novel lie.

On Chesil Beach is packed with all the period detail one might expect, and occasionally it can feel as though McEwan's working off a checklist; there's the bad food, the CND marches, the naïveté about the Soviet Union, the social-realist movies, the Beatles and the Stones…. Hold on a minute. The Beatles and the Stones? "He played her 'clumsy but honourable' cover versions of Chuck Berry songs by the Beatles and the Rolling Stones." Well, not before July 1962 he didn't. (The sentence refers to the couple's courtship.) What's strange about this anachronism is that McEwan must, at some stage, have thought of the Larkin poem when he was writing this—it might even have inspired him in some way. So if the Beatles' first LP was released in the same year sexual intercourse was invented, what exactly was he playing her in the months leading up to July 1962? "Love Me Do" was released toward the end of that year, and there was nothing else recorded yet; the Stones, meanwhile, didn't produce anything until the following year. Does it matter? It didn't affect my enjoyment of the book, but I suspect that it does, a little. The Beatles really did belong to a different age, metaphorically and literally. I hereby offer my services as a full-time researcher.

On Chesil Beach is so short that it's actually hard to talk about without revealing more than you might want to know. You should read it, and be thankful that you grew up in a different age, where all matters sexual were a whole lot easier. Too easy, probably. Some of you younger ones are probably having sex now, absentmindedly, while reading this. You probably don't even know that you're having sex. You'll look down or up at the end of this paragraph and think, Eeek! Who's that? Well, that can't be right, can it? Surely things have gone too far the other way, if that's what's happening? I'm off to read some Jane Austen. ✱

AUGUST 2007

BOOKS BOUGHT:
* The Ha-Ha—Jennifer Dawson
* Poppy Shakespeare—Clare Allan
* Yo, Blair!—Geoffrey Wheatcroft
* Salmon Fishing in the Yemen—Paul Torday
* The Myth of the Blitz—Angus Calder
* This Book Will Save Your Life—A. M. Homes

BOOKS READ:
* Across the Great Divide: The Band and America—Barney Hoskyns
* Stasiland: Stories from Behind the Berlin Wall—Anna Funder
* Yo, Blair!—Geoffrey Wheatcroft
* The Ha-Ha—Jennifer Dawson
* Coming Through Slaughter—Michael Ondaatje
* Poppy Shakespeare—Clare Allan

On the face of it, the Stasi and the Band had very little in common. Closer examination, however, reveals the East German secret police force and the brilliant genre-fusing Canadian rock group to be surprisingly... Oh, forget it. I don't have to do that stuff in this column—or at least, if I do, nobody has ever told me. It goes without saying that the two wires that led me to the books by Barney Hoskyns and Anna Funder came from different sockets in the soul, and power completely different, you know, electrical/spiritual devices: *Stasiland* and *Across the Great Divide* are as different as a hair dryer and a Hoover. Yes. That's it. I'm the first to admit it when my metaphors don't work, but I'm pretty sure I pulled that one off. (I wish I'd hated them both. Then I could have said that one sucks, and the other blows. Regrettably, they were pretty good.)

The journey/length of cable that led me to the Hoskyns book began a couple of years ago, when I was just about to walk out of a music club. We'd gone to see the support act, but the headliners had this amazing young guitar player called James Walbourne, an unearthly cross between James Burton, Peter Green, and Richard Thompson; Walbourne's fluid, tasteful, beautiful solos drop the jaw, stop the heart, and smack the gob, all at the same time. We still walked out of the club, because we really wanted a pizza, and pizza always beats art, but I was determined to track him down and make sure that I hadn't been imagining it all. I've seen him a few times since; when he's not playing with the Pernice Brothers or Son Volt or Tift Merritt, he's been appearing with his own band in a pub not far from me. And he's recently taken to playing a cover of the Band's "Ain't No More Cane," a song off *The Basement Tapes.* So then I had a fit on the Band—I have pretty much listened to every single track on the box set that came out last year—and then I noticed that I had an unread 1993 biography on my shelves. Before long I was being taken from Stratford, Ontario, to the Mississippi Delta and on to Los Angeles.

In one crucial way, writing about the Band is difficult: Greil Marcus got there first, in his book *Mystery Train,* and Marcus's essay is still the best piece of rock criticism I have ever read. (There are thirty-seven separate index entries for Greil Marcus in *Across the Great Divide,* and yet Hoskyns still feels it necessary to get sniffy about a couple of factual errors that Marcus made in his writings. You'd have hoped that Hoskyns could have been more forgiving, seeing as how his own book would have been a lot shorter without Marcus's help.) And yet there's something irresistible about the story too, because it's the story of white rock and roll. Here's Robbie Robertson, age sixteen, getting on a train and heading down to

the American South from Canada, to play R&B covers with Ron-
nie Hawkins's Hawks; Robertson's pilgrimage from white Sleepy-
town to the birthplace of the blues was the one that millions of
teenage guitarists made, in their heads at least, at the beginning of
the '60s. (It may even still go on. I would imagine that James Walbourne has made exactly the same trip, and maybe not even sym-
bolically. He lives in Muswell Hill, north London, which is sort of
like Canada.) And here's Robbie Robertson, in his early thirties,
bombed out of his head on cocaine, living with Martin Scorsese
in a house on Mulholland Drive that had blackout covers on the
windows so that the residents no longer knew or cared whether it
was day or night. That, in a nutshell, is what happened to our music between the early '60s and the mid-'70s: the geographical shift,
the decadence, and the obliviousness to the outside world. Thank
heaven for punk. And Abba.

I may be the only person in the world who has just read *Across
the Great Divide* after seeing James Walbourne play "Ain't No More
Cane." I can't imagine I'm the only person in the world who has
read *Stasiland* after seeing *The Lives of Others* in my local cinema.
I left that film wanting to know more about the chilling weirdness
of life in the old GDR, and Anna Funder's brilliant book is full of
stories that not only leave you openmouthed at the sheer luna-
tic ambition of the totalitarian experiment but break your heart as
well, just as they should do.

Funder reviewed *The Lives of Others* in a recent issue of *Sight
and Sound,* and argued persuasively that, while it was a great film
on its own terms, it bore little resemblance to life as it was lived behind the Berlin Wall: the movie was too bloodless, and there never
was and never could be such a thing as a heroic Stasi officer. Her
book is personal and anecdotal: she tells the stories she has come
across, some of which she discovers when she places an advertise-
ment in a local newspaper in an attempt to contact former Stasi
members. This approach is perfect, because you don't need any-

thing other than personal anecdote to tell a kind of truth about the Stasi. They knew everybody—that was the point of them. So who wouldn't have a story to tell?

I'd be doing you and the book a disservice if I recommended it to you simply as an outstanding work of contemporary history. I'm guessing that a fair few of you are writers, and one of the unexpected strengths of this book is the implausibility of the narratives Funder unearths—narratives that nevertheless, and contrary to all perceived wisdom, seem to resonate with, and illuminate, and illustrate even greater truths. Frau Paul gives birth to a desperately sick baby just as the Wall is being built; one morning she wakes up to find that it has separated her from the only hospital that can help her son. Doctors smuggle him, without her permission, over the Wall. He lives in the hospital for the next five years.

Frau Paul is given only agonizingly sporadic permission to visit her child, and she and her husband decide, perhaps not unnaturally, that they will try to escape to West Berlin. Their plans are discovered; Frau Paul refuses to cut a deal that will endanger a young man in the West who has been helping her and others. She is sent to prison. Her son is nearly five years old when he is finally allowed home. (It's interesting, incidentally, that the central characters in *The Lives of Others* are all childless. I suspect children tend to limit the range of moral choices.)

There are, it seems, stories like this on every street corner of the old East Germany, insane stories, stories that defy belief and yet unfold with a terrible logic, and Anna Funder's weary credulity, and her unerring eye for the unimaginable varieties of irony to be found in a world like this, make her the perfect narrator. Believe it or not, there are some funny bits.

It was our prime minister's tenth anniversary recently, and by the time you get to read this he'll be gone anyway, so it seemed appropriate to give him a little bit of consideration. Not much—Geoffrey Wheatcroft's polemic is only 120-odd pages long—

but the time it took me to read it was precisely the sort of time I wanted to give him. The title, *Yo, Blair!* refers to your president's form of address during the disastrously revealing conversation Blair had with Bush during the G8 meeting in Russia last year, when an open mic revealed the true nature of their relationship to be something closer to the one between Jeeves and Bertie Wooster than that between two world leaders, although obviously Jeeves was less servile.

Wheatcroft overstates his case a little: however much you hate Blair, it's hard to hear that his soppy Third Way contains under-tones of the Third Reich. But when you see the crimes and mis-demeanors piled up like this, it's hard to see how we managed to avoid foreign invaders intent on regime change. It's not just Iraq and the special relationship with the U.S., although it's quite clear now that this is how Blair will be remembered. It's the sucking up to the rich and powerful (Berlusconi, Cliff Richard), the freeload-ing, the pathetic little lies, the broken promises, the apparent ab-sence of any sort of conviction, beyond the conviction of his own rectitude. This book introduced me to a very handy word, *antino-mian*. (Oh, come on. Give me a break. I can't know everything. Where would I put it? And think of all the other hundreds of words I've used in this column.) You are antinomian, apparently, when your own sense of self-righteousness allows you to do any-thing, however mean or vicious or morally bankrupt that thing might appear to be. It's been a while, one suspects, since this word could be legitimately applied to a world leader; even Nixon and Kissinger may have slept uneasily for a couple of nights after they bombed Cambodia.

Here is the best definition of a good novel I have come across yet—indeed, I suspect that it might be the only definition of a good novel worth a damn. A good novel is one that sends you scurrying to the computer to look at pictures of prostitutes on the Internet. And as Michael Ondaatje's *Coming Through Slaughter* is the only novel I have ever read that has made me do this, I can confidently assert that *Coming Through Slaughter* is, ipso facto, the best novel I have ever read.

Regrettably, the pictures in question are by E. J. Bellocq, a central character in *Coming Through Slaughter,* which means that they have a great deal of redeeming cultural import (Susan Sontag wrote a brilliant introduction to a published collection of his work); when I read a novel that allows me to ransack the Internet for prostitute pictures willy-nilly, this column will be awarding a prize worth more than any genius grant.

I had been having some trouble with the whole idea of fiction, trouble that seemed in some way connected with my recent landmark birthday; it seemed to me that a lot of novels were, to be blunt, *made up,* and could teach me little about the world. Life suddenly seemed so short that I needed facts, and I needed them fast. I picked up *Coming Through Slaughter* in the spirit of kill or cure, and I was cured—I have only read fiction since I finished it. It's sort of ironic, then, that Ondaatje's novel ended up introducing me to an important photographer, anyway. (Oh, come on. Give me a break. I can't know everyone. Where would I put them? And think of all the other... No, you're right. You can only use this argument seven or eight hundred times before it begins to sound pathetic.)

Coming Through Slaughter, Ondaatje's first novel, is an extraordinary, and extraordinarily beautiful, piece of mythmaking, a short, rich imagining of the life of Buddy Bolden, a New Orleans cornettist widely regarded as one of the founders of jazz. It seems to me as though anybody who has doubts about the value of fiction should read this book: it leaves you with the sort of ache that nonfiction can never provide, and provides an intensity and glow that are the unique product of a singular imagination laying its gauze over the brilliant light of the world. Ondaatje writes about the music wonderfully well: you couldn't ask for anyone better to describe the sound of the crack that must happen when one form is being bent too far out of shape in an attempt to form something else. And Bolden's madness—he is supposed to have collapsed during a carnival procession—provides endless interesting corridors for Ondaatje to wander around in. I am still thinking about this novel, remembering the heat it threw off, weeks after finishing it.

I am a literal-minded and simple soul, so since then I have read nothing but novels about mentally ill people. If it worked once, I reasoned, then there's no reason why it shouldn't work every time, and I was right. I have now taken a broad enough sample, and I can reveal that nobody has ever written a bad novel about insanity.

This is strange, if you think about it. You'd think the subject would give all sorts of people disastrous scope to write indulgent, carefully fucked-up prose asking us to think about whether the insane are actually more sane than the rest of us. Both Jennifer Dawson's *The Ha-Ha* and Clare Allan's *Poppy Shakespeare* miraculously avoid this horrible cliché; to crudify both of these terrific books, the line they take is that people suffering from a mental illness are more mentally ill than people who are not suffering from a mental illness. This, given the general use the subject is put to in popular culture, is something of a relief.

The Ha-Ha is a lost novel from 1961, recently championed by the English writer Susan Hill on her blog; *Poppy Shakespeare* was first published last year. Both are first novels, both are set in institutions, and both are narrated by young females attached to these institutions. *The Ha-Ha* is quieter, more conventional, partly because Jennifer Dawson's heroine is an Oxford graduate who speaks in a careful, if necessarily neurotic, Oxford prose. Clare Allan's N is a brilliant fictional creation whose subordinate clauses tumble over each other in an undisciplined, glorious rush of north London energy. I liked them both, but I loved *Poppy Shakespeare*. It's not often you finish a first novel by a writer and you are seized by the need to read her second immediately. Of course, by the time her second comes out, I'll have forgotten all about the first. But today, the will is there.

Anyway, hurrah for fiction! Down with facts! Facts are for the dull, and the straight, and the old! You'll never find out anything about the world through facts! I might, however, have a look at this Brian Clough biography I've just been sent. Football doesn't count, does it? ✭

SEPTEMBER 2007

BOOKS BOUGHT:

* *Skellig*—David Almond
* *Clay*—David Almond
* *Tom's Midnight Garden*—
  Philippa Pearce
* *Queuing for Beginners:
  The Story of Daily Life
  from Breakfast
  to Bedtime*—Joe Moran
* *The Road*—Cormac
  McCarthy
* *Better: A Surgeon's Notes
  on Performance*—
  Atul Gawande
* *The Rights of the
  Reader*—Daniel Pennac

BOOKS READ:

* *Skellig*—David Almond
* *Clay*—David Almond
* *Sharp Teeth*—
  Toby Barlow
* *The Road*—Cormac
  McCarthy
* *The Brambles*—
  Eliza Minot
* *Queuing for Beginners*—
  Joe Moran
* *American Born Chinese*—
  Gene Luen Yang

I had all sorts of clever introductions to this month's column written in my head, opening paragraphs that would have provoked and inspired and maybe even amused one or two of you, if you were in a really good mood. When I read the Eliza Minot novel, I started working up this riff about the joys of uncannily accurate impersonation; when I read the David Almond novels, I was going to tell you all to abandon adult fiction and turn to books written for kids and teenagers. And then I read the Cormac McCarthy novel, and they all seemed inappropriate, like trying to tell New Yorkers about my news first on September 11, 2001.

As you probably know by now—and more than eight million

of you voted for it in the Believer Book Award—*The Road* may well be the most miserable book ever written, and God knows there's some competition out there. Two survivors of the apocalypse, a man and his young son, wander through the scarred gray landscape foraging for food, and trying to avoid the feral gangs who would rather kill them and eat them than share their sandwiches with them. The man spends much of the book wondering whether he should shoot his son with their last remaining bullet, just to spare him any further pain. Sometimes they find unexpected caches of food and drink. Sometimes they find shriveled heads, or the remains of a baby on a barbecue. Sometimes you feel like begging the man to use his last bullet on you, rather than the boy. The boy is a fictional creation, after all, but you're not. You're really suffering. Reading *The Road* is rather like attending the beautiful funeral of someone you love who has died young. You're happy that the ceremony seems to be going so well, and you know you'll remember the experience for the rest of your life, but the truth is that you'd rather not be there at all.

What do we think about when we read a novel this distressing? *The Road* is a brilliant book, but it is not a complicated one, so it's not as if we can distract ourselves with contemplation; you respond mostly with your gut rather than your mind. My wife, who read it just before I did, has vowed to become more practical in order to prepare herself for the end of the world; her lack of culinary imagination when handed a few wizened animal gizzards and some old bits of engine has left her with the feeling that she'd be an inadequate mother if worse comes to worst. And I ended up thinking about those occasional articles about the death of the novel—almost by definition, seeing as our planet hasn't yet suffered this kind of fatal trauma, you cannot find a nonfiction book as comprehensively harrowing or as provocative as this. Most of the time, however, you just experience an agonizing empathy, especially, perhaps, if you are a parent, and you end up wondering what you can possibly do with it, apart from carry it around with you for days afterward. "It is also a warning," one of the reviews quoted on the back of my paperback tells me. Well, after reading this, I definitely won't be pushing the button that brings about the global holocaust.

It is important to remember that *The Road* is a product of one man's imagination: the literary world has a tendency to believe that the least consoling worldview is the Truth. (How many times have you read someone describe a novel as "unflinching," in approving terms? What's wrong with a little flinch every once in a while?) McCarthy is true to his own vision, which is what gives his novel its awesome power. But maybe when Judgment Day does come, we'll surprise each other by sharing our sandwiches and singing "Bridge over Troubled Water" rather than by scooping out our children's brains with spoons. Yes, it's the job of artists to force us to stare at the horror until we're on the verge of passing out. But it's also the job of artists to offer warmth and hope and maybe even an escape from lives that can occasionally seem unendurably drab. I wouldn't want to pick one job over the other—they both seem pretty important to me. And it's quite legitimate, I think, not to want to read *The Road*. There are some images now embedded in my memory that I don't especially want there. Don't let anyone tell you that you have a *duty* to read it.

So here's the introduction about mimicry. It goes something like this. Ahem. Believe it or not, I am not a good mimic. I can only do one impersonation, an actually pretty passable stab at Mick Jagger, *but only as he appears in the* Simpsons *episode in which Homer goes to rock and roll fantasy camp*. It's not much, I admit, but it's mine, and when I pull it off, my children laugh—simply, I guess, because it sounds so like the original, rather than because I am doing anything funny. (I never do anything funny.) Some of the considerable pleasure I drew from Eliza Minot's *The Brambles* came from her enviable ability to capture family life with such precision that... Well, you don't want to laugh, exactly, because *The Brambles* is mostly about how three adult siblings cope with a dying father, but there is something about Minot's facility that engenders a kind of child-like delight: How did she *do* that? Do it again! One conversation in particular, in which a mother is attempting to explain the mysteries of death to her young children, is so loving in its depiction of the mess you can get into in these situations, and so uncannily authentic, that you end up resenting the amount of inauthentic claptrap you consume during your reading life. *The Brambles* isn't perfect—there's a plot twist that ends up overloading the narrative without giving the book anything much in return—but Eliza Minot is clearly on the verge of producing something special.

It's been a pretty significant reading month, now that I think about it. I read a modern classic that took away whatever will to live I have left, discovered a couple of younger writers, and then came across an unfamiliar genre that, I suspect, will prove of great significance for both my reading and my writing life. I recently completed my first novel for or possibly just about young adults, and my U.S. publishers asked me to go to Washington, D.C., to read from and talk about the book to an audience of librarians. One of the writers on the panel with me was a guy called David Almond, whose work I didn't know; a couple of days before I met him, his novel *Skellig* was voted the third greatest children's book of the last seventy years. (Philip Pullman's *Northern Lights* was top, and Philippa Pearce's *Tom's Midnight Garden* came in second.)

I read *Skellig* on the plane, and though I have no idea whether it's the third greatest children's book of the last seventy years, I can tell you that it's one of the best novels published in the last decade, and I'd never heard of it. Have you? *Skellig* is the beautifully simple and bottomlessly complicated story of a boy who finds a sick angel in his garage, a stinking, croaking creature who loves Chinese take-aways and brown ale. Meanwhile, Michael's baby sister lies desperately sick in a hospital, fluttering gently between life and death.

The only problem with reading *Skellig* at an advanced age is that it's over before you know it; a twelve-year-old might be able to eke it out, spend a little longer in the exalted, downbeat world that Almond creates. *Skellig* is a children's book because it is accessible and because it has children at the center of its narrative, but, believe me, it's for you too, because it's for everybody, and the author knows it. At one point, Mina, Michael's friend, a next-door neighbor who is being homeschooled, picks up one of Michael's books and flicks through it.

"Yeah, looks good," she said. "But what's the red sticker for?"

"It's for confident readers," I said. "It's to do with reading age."

"And what if other readers wanted to read it?... And where would William Blake fit in?... 'Tyger! Tyger! Burning bright / In the forests of the night.' Is that for the best readers or the worst readers? Does it need a good reading age?... And if it was for the worst readers would the best readers not bother with it because it was too stupid for them?"

Now that I think about it, Mina's observations might well summarize what this column has been attempting to say all along.

For the first time in the last three or four years, I read two books in a row by the same author, and though *Clay* isn't quite as elegant as *Skellig,* it's still extraordinary, a piece of pre-Christian mythmaking set in the northeast of England in the late '60s. And suddenly, I'm aware that there may well be scores of authors like David Almond, people producing masterpieces that I am ignorant of because I happen to be older than the intended readership. Is *The Road* better than *Skellig?* That wouldn't be a very interesting argument. But when I'd finished *Clay* I read an adult novel, a thriller, that was meretricious, dishonest, pretentious, disastrously constructed, and garlanded with gushing reviews; in other words, the best readers had spoken.

Meanwhile, the hits just kept on coming. Gene Luen Yang's *American Born Chinese* is a clever, crisply drawn graphic novel about the embarrassment of almost belonging; Toby Barlow's *Sharp Teeth* is a novel about werewolves in Los Angeles, and it's written in blank verse, and it's tremendous. I can't remember now if I've ever cried wolf, as it were, and recommended other blank-verse werewolf novels—probably I have. Well, forget them all, because this is the one.

I was sent a proof copy of *Sharp Teeth,* and when I saw it, I wished it well, but couldn't imagine actually reading it, what with it being a blank-verse novel about werewolves and all. But I looked at the first page, got to the bottom of it, turned it over, read the second page, and… You get the picture, anyway. You're all smart people, and you know the conventional way to get through a book. All I'm saying is that my desire to persist took me by surprise.

I had suspected that *Sharp Teeth* might not be serious—that it would turn out to be a satire about the film industry, for example (sharp teeth, L.A., agents, producers, blah blah). But the beauty of the book is that it's deadly serious; like David Almond, Toby Barlow takes his mythical creatures literally, and lets the narrative provide the metaphor. It's stomach-churningly violent in places (they don't mess around, werewolves, do they?), and tender, and satisfyingly complicated: there's an involved plot about rival gangs that lends the book a great deal of noir cool. The blank verse does precisely what Barlow must have hoped it would do, namely, add intensity without distracting, or affecting readability. And it's as ambitious as any literary novel, because underneath all that fur, it's about identity, community, love, death, and all the things we want our books to be about. I'm not quite sure how Barlow can follow this, if he wants to. But there's every chance that *Sharp Teeth* will end up being clasped to the collective bosom of the young, dark, and fucked-up.

It seems years ago now that I dipped into Joe Moran's engaging *Queuing for Beginners: The Story of Daily Life from Breakfast to Bedtime*. Externally, I have only aged a month or so since I picked it up, but in the meantime I have endured an Altamont of the mind, and my soul feels five hundred years old. Post McCarthy, it's hard to remember those carefree days when I could engross myself in anecdotes about the Belisha beacon, and short social histories of commuting and the cigarette break. (Eighty-nine percent of Englishmen smoked in 1949! And we were still a proper world power back then! My case rests.) And I suppose a sense of purpose and hope might return, slowly, if I read enough P. G. Wodehouse and sports biographies. I have nearly finished the Joe Moran, and I would very much like to read his final chapter about the duvet. But what's the point, really? There won't be duvets in the future, you know. And if there are, they will be needed to cover the putrefying bodies of our families. Is there anything funny on TV? ✷

OCTOBER 2007

The story so far: I have written a young-adult novel, and on a trip to Washington, D.C., to promote it, I met a load of librarians and other assorted enthusiasts who introduced me to a magical new world that I knew nothing about. I really do feel as though I've walked through the back of a wardrobe into some parallel universe, peopled by amazing writers whom you never seem to read about on books pages, and who never come up in conversations with literary friends. (The truth, I suspect, is that these writers are frequently written about on books pages, and I have never bothered to read the reviews; come to think of it, they probably come up frequently in conversations with literary friends, and I have never bothered to listen to anything these friends say.)

It was in D.C. that I met David Almond, whose brilliant book *Skellig* started me off on this YA jag; and it was in D.C. that Francesca Lia Block's *Weetzie Bat*, first published in 1989, was frequently cited as something that started something, although to begin with, I wasn't sure what *Weetzie Bat* was, or even if the people talking about it were speaking in a language I understood, so I can't, unfortunately, tell you what *Weetzie Bat* is responsible for. When I got home, I bought it from Amazon (it doesn't seem to be available in the U.K.), and a few days later I received a very tiny paperback, 113 large-print pages long and about three inches high, and suspiciously, intimidatingly pink. Pink! And gold! The book is so short that you really don't need to be seen with it on public transport, but I wouldn't have cared anyway, because it's beautiful, and I would have defended its honor against any football hooligan who wanted to snigger at me.

Weetzie Bat is, I suppose, about single mothers and AIDS and homosexuality and loneliness, but that's like saying that "Desolation Row" is about Cinderella and Einstein and Bette Davis. And actually, when I was trying to recall the last time I was exposed to a mind this singular, it was Dylan's book *Chronicles* that I thought of—not because Block thinks or writes in a similar way, and she certainly doesn't write or think about similar things, but because this kind of originality in prose is very rare indeed. Most of the time we comprehend the imagination and intellect behind the novels we read, even when that intellect is more powerful than our own—you can admire and enjoy Philip Roth, for example, but I don't believe that anyone has ever finished *American Pastoral* and thought, Where the hell did that come from? *Weetzie Bat* is not *American Pastoral* (and it's not "Desolation Row"—or *Great Expectations,* while we're at it), but it's genuinely eccentric, and picking it up for the first time is like coming across a chocolate fountain in the middle of the desert. You might not feel like diving in, but you would certainly be curious about the decision-making process of the person who put it there.

Weetzie Bat is a young woman, and she lives in a Day-Glo, John Waters–camp version of Los Angeles. Eventually she meets the love of her life, whose name is My Secret Agent Lover Man, and they have a baby called Cherokee, and they adopt another one called Witch Baby, and... You know what? A synopsis isn't really going to do this book justice. If you've never heard of it (and of the six people questioned in the Spree offices, only one knew what I was talking about), and you want to spend about eighty-three minutes on an entirely different planet, then this is the book for you.

I read *Tom's Midnight Garden* because it finished one place above *Skellig* in a list of the greatest Carnegie Medalists of all time. (Phillipa Pearce's classic came runner-up to Philip Pullman. I'm sure the Pullman is great, but it will be a while before I am persuaded that sprites and hobbits and third universes are for me, although I'm all for the death of God.) Like everything else in this genre, apparently, it is a work of genius, although unlike *Weetzie Bat* or *Skellig,* it is unquestionably a story for children, and at the halfway mark, I was beginning to feel as though I might finish it without feeling that my life had been profoundly enriched. I mean, I could see that it was great and so on, but I was wondering whether my half century on the planet might be cushioning me from the full impact. But at the end of the book—and you've been able to see the twist coming from miles away, yet there's not a damned thing you can do to stop it from slaying you—I'm not ashamed to say that I cr... Actually, I am ashamed to say that. It's a book about a kid who finds a magic garden at the back of his aunt's house, and there's no way a grown man should be doing that.

They've been very disorienting, these last few weeks. I see now that dismissing YA books because you're not a young adult is a little bit like refusing to watch thrillers on the grounds that you're not a policeman or a dangerous criminal, and as a consequence, I've discovered a previously ignored room at the back of the bookstore that's filled with masterpieces I've never heard of,

the YA equivalents of *The Maltese Falcon* and *Strangers on a Train.*
Weirdly, then, reading YA stuff now is a little like being a young
adult way back then: Is this Vonnegut guy any good? What about
Albert Camus? Anyone ever heard of him? The world suddenly
seems a larger place.

And there's more to this life-changing D.C. trip. While I was
there, I learned about something called the Alex Awards, a list of
ten adult books that the Young Adult Library Services Association
believes will appeal to younger readers, and I became peculiarly—
perhaps inappropriately—excited by the idea. Obviously this award
is laudable and valuable and all that, but my first thought was this:
You mean, every year someone publishes a list of ten adult books
that are compelling enough for teenagers? In other words, a list of
ten books *that aren't boring?* Let me at it. I bought two of this year's
nominees, Michael D'Orso's *Eagle Blue* and Ron Rash's *The World
Made Straight,* having noticed that another of the ten was Michael
Lewis's brilliant book about your football, *The Blind Side: Evolution
of a Game,* and a fourth was David Mitchell's *Black Swan Green,*
which I haven't read but which friends love. Whoever compiled
this list knew what they were talking about. Who else might have
won an Alex Award? Dickens, surely, for *Great Expectations* and
David Copperfield; Donna Tartt, for *The Secret History;* Dodie Smith's
I Capture the Castle. Probably *Pride and Prejudice* and *Le Grand
Meaulnes. This Boy's Life,* certainly, and *The Liar's Club,* Roddy
Doyle for *Paddy Clarke Ha Ha Ha...* In other words, if a book
couldn't have made that list, then it's probably not worth reading.

Like every other paperback, Rash's book comes elaborately
decorated with admiring quotes from reviews. Unlike every other
paperback, however, his Alex nomination gave me confidence in
them. "A beautifully rendered palimpsest," said *BookPage,* and I'd
have to say that this wouldn't entice me, normally. You can see
how a book could be a beautifully rendered palimpsest and yet
somehow remain on the dull side. But the Alex allowed me to
insert the words *and not boring* at the end of the quote. "Graceful,
conscientious prose," said the *Charlotte Observer—and yet not bor-*

ing. "Rash writes with beauty and simplicity, understanding his characters with a poet's eye and heart and telling their tales with a poet's tongue, *and not boring people rigid while he does it,*" said William Gay, almost. You see how it works? It's fantastic.

And *The World Made Straight* really is engrossing—indeed, the last devastating fifty-odd pages are almost too compelling. You want to look away, but you can't, and as a consequence you have to watch while some bad men get what was coming to them, and a flawed, likable man gets what you hoped he might avoid. It's a satisfyingly complicated story about second chances and history and education and the relationships between parents and their children; it's violent, real, very well written, and it moves like a train.

When I was reading it, I ended up trying to work out how some complicated novels seem small, claustrophobic, beside the point, sometimes even without a point, while others take off into the fresh air that all the great books seem to breathe. There would be plenty of ways of turning this book, with its drug deals and its Civil War backstory, into something too knotty to live—sometimes writers are so caught up in being true to the realities of their characters' lives that they seem to forget that they have to be true to ours too, however tangentially. Rash, however, manages to convince you right from the first page that his characters and his story are going to matter to you, even if you live in north London rather than on a tobacco farm in North Carolina; it's an enviable skill, and it's demonstrated here so confidently, and with such a lack of show, that you almost forget Rash has it until it's too late, and your own sense of well-being is bound up in the fate of the characters. Bad mistake, almost. There is some redemption here, but it's real redemption, hard-won and fragile rather than sappy. *The World Made Straight* was a fantastic introduction to the Not Boring Awards. I was, I admit, a little concerned that these books might be a little too uplifting, and would wear their lessons and morals on their T-shirts, but this one at least is hard and powerful, and it refuses to judge people that some moral guardians might feel need judging.

Lawrence Weschler's *Everything That Rises: A Book of Converg-*

ences is never going to be nominated for an Alex, I fear. Not because it's boring—it isn't—but it's dense, and allusive, by definition, and Weschler's thinking is angular, subtle, dizzying. I feel as though I only just recently became old enough to read it, so you lot will have to wait twenty or thirty years.

It's worth it, though. You know you're in for a treat right from the very first essay, in which Weschler interviews the Ground Zero photographer Joel Meyerowitz about the uncanny compositional similarities between his photos and a whole slew of other works of art. How come Meyerowitz's shot of the devastated Winter Garden in the World Trade Center looks exactly like one of Piranesi's imaginary prisons? Is it pure coincidence? Or conscious design? It turns out, of course, to be something in between, something much more interesting than either of these explanations, and in working toward the truth of it, Weschler produces more grounded observations about the production of art than you'd believe possible, given the apparently whimsical nature of the exercise.

And he does this time and time again with his "convergences." No, you think in the first few lines of every one of these essays. Stop it. You are not going to be able to persuade me that Oliver Sacks's *Awakenings* can tell us anything about the recent history of Eastern Europe. Or: no, Newt Gingrich and Slobodan Milošević have nothing in common, and I won't listen to you trying to argue otherwise. You got away with it last time, but this is too much. And then by the end of the piece, you feel stupid for not noticing it yourself, and you want Gingrich tried for war crimes. It's an incredibly rewarding read, part magic, part solid but inspired close practical criticism, and the best book about (mostly) art I've come across since Dave Hickey's mighty *Air Guitar*. When I'd finished *Everything That Rises* I felt cleverer—not just because I knew more, but because I felt it would help me to think more creatively about other things. In fact, I've just pitched an idea to Weschler's editor about the weird chimes between the departure of Thierry Henry from Arsenal and the last days of Nicolae Ceausescu, but so far, no word. I think I might have blown his mind. ✻

NOVEMBER/
DECEMBER 2007

BOOKS BOUGHT:
* *The Pigman*—Paul Zindel
* *The Bethlehem Murders*—
  Matt Rees
* *The Dud Avocado*—
  Elaine Dundy
* *Singled Out*—
  Virginia Nicholson

BOOKS READ:
* *Holes*—Louis Sachar
* *The Fall-Out: How a Guilty
  Liberal Lost His Innocence*—
  Andrew Anthony
* *A Disorder Peculiar to
  the Country*—Ken Kalfus
* *Seeing Is Forgetting the Name
  of the Thing One Sees: A Life
  of Contemporary Artist Robert
  Irwin*—Lawrence Weschler
  (unfinished)
* *Bridge of Sighs*—
  Richard Russo (unfinished)

Weirdly, I have had sackfuls of letters from *Believer* readers recently asking me—*begging* me—to imagine my reading month as a cake. I can only imagine that young people in America find things easier to picture if they are depicted in some kind of edible form, and, though one cannot help but find this troubling, in the end I value literacy more highly than health; if our two countries were full of fat readers, rather than millions of Victoria Beckhams, then we would all be better off.

As luck would have it, this was the perfect month to institute the cake analogies. The reading cake divided neatly in half, with Andrew Anthony's *The Fall-Out* and Ken Kalfus's *A Disorder*

Peculiar to the Country, both inspired by 9/11, on one plate, and Richard Russo's *Bridge of Sighs* and Lawrence Weschler's biography of the artist Robert Irwin on the other. Louis Sachar's *Holes,* meanwhile, is a kind of nonattributable, indivisible cherry on the top. There. Happy now? I'm warning you: it might not work that satisfactorily every month.

Andrew Anthony is a former five-a-side football teammate of mine (he still plays, but my hamstrings have forced me into a tragically premature retirement), a leggy, tough-tackling midfielder whose previous book was a little meditation on penalty kicks. I'm not underestimating Andy's talent when I say that this book is a top-corner, thirty-yard volley out of the blue; you're always surprised, I suspect, when someone you know chiefly through sport produces a timely, pertinent, and brilliantly argued book about the crisis in left-liberalism, unless you share a season ticket with Noam Chomsky, or Eric Hobsbawm is your goalkeeper.

Anthony (and if he wants a future in this business, he's got to get himself a surname) is a few years younger than me, but we have more or less the same political memories and touchstones: the miners' strike in the mid-'80s, the earnest discussions about feminism that took place around the same time, the unexamined assumption that the U.S.A. was just as much an enemy of freedom as the Soviet Union. *Liberalism* was a dirty word, just as it is in your country now, but in our case it was because liberals were softies who didn't want to smash the State. As Anthony points out, we would have been in a right state if anyone had smashed the State—most of us were dependent on the university grants or the dole money that the State gave us, but never mind. We wanted it gone. These views were commonplace among students and graduates in the 1980s; there were at least as many people who wanted to smash the State as there were people who wanted to listen to Haircut 100.

Anthony took it further than most. He read a lot of unreadable Marxist pamphlets, and went to Nicaragua to help out the Sandinistas. (I would have gone, but what with one thing and another, the decade just seemed to slip by. And also: I know this keeps coming up, but what are you supposed to do when there's a revolution on and you're a season-ticket holder at a football club? Just, like, not go to the games?) He also had it tougher than most: Anthony was a working-class boy whose early childhood was spent in a house without a bath or an indoor toilet—a common enough experience in the Britain of the 1930s and '40s, much rarer in the '60s and '70s. The things you learn about your friends when they write memoirs, eh? He had every right to sign up for a bit of class warfare. In the wearyingly inevitable name-calling that has accompanied the publication of his book, he has been called a "middle-class twat."

Anthony, however, has concluded that the class war is now being fought only by the deluded and those so entrenched in the old ideologies that they have lost the power of reason. Which economic and political system would we really prefer? Which economic system would the working class prefer? Which economic system gives women the best chance of fulfilling their potential? Nobody, least of all Anthony, is suggesting that the free market should go unchecked—that's why liberalism still matters. Post 9/11, however, all that Old Left aggression, now whizzing round with nowhere to go, is being spent not on Iran, or North Korea, or any of the other countries that make their citizens' lives a misery, but on the U.S.—not your hapless president, but the place, the people, the idea. Anthony threads some of the most egregious quotes from liberal-left writers throughout the book, and when you see them gathered together like that, these writers remind you of nothing so much as a bunch of drunks at closing time, muttering gibberish and swinging their fists at anyone who comes remotely close. "It has become painfully clear that most Americans simply don't get it," wrote one on September 13, 2001 (which, as Anthony points out, means that he would have had to have finished his copy exactly twenty-four hours after the Twin Towers fell). "Shock, rage and grief there have been aplenty. But any glimmer of recognition of why.... the United States is hated with such bitterness.... seems almost entirely absent." Yes, well. Give them another day or so to get over the shock and grief, and they're bound to come round to your way of thinking. "When I look at the U.K., it reminds me of the Nazi era," said another, apparently in all seriousness. "While the killing of innocent people is to be condemned without question, there is something rather repugnant about those who rush to renounce acts of terrorism," said a third. (Are these rushers more or less repugnant than the acts of terrorism themselves? It's hard to tell.) By the time you get to the Index on Censorship editorial asking us to "applaud Theo van Gogh's death as the marvellous piece of theatre it was," you start to wonder whether some of these people might actually be clinically insane. Van Gogh, you may remember, was the Dutch filmmaker who was shot eight times and had his throat cut to the spine in broad daylight on a busy Amsterdam street. His last words were "Can't we talk about this?" How's that for censorship?

Sometimes, the doublethink necessary to produce observations and opinions like these can only produce disbelieving laughter. My favorite comic moment is provided by a leading Afro-Caribbean commentator, writing about the Asian immigrants expelled from Uganda by Idi Amin: "The Asians from Uganda came to what can only be described as the most inhospitable country on earth." The country he's talking about, of course, is Britain, the place the Asians fled to. This cannot literally be true, can it? However fierce our self-loathing, we must concede that, in this context at least, we came in a disappointing second place in the Most Inhospitable Country on Earth Cup. Uganda, the country that took everything the Ugandan Asians owned and forced them out under threat of death, won the gold medal fair and square.

This book has inevitably been misunderstood by many on the left as some kind of revisionist right-wing diatribe. It's true that Anthony owns up to believing in causes and systems that slowly revealed themselves to have been unworthy of anyone's belief, but this is an inevitable part of getting older. But *The Fall-Out* is really about the slippery relativist slope that leads tolerant, intelligent people to defend the right of unintelligent and intolerant people to be intolerant in ways that cannot help but damage a free society; I think we do a lot more of that in the U.K. than you do over there, possibly because the only people who have any real belief in an idea of England—invariably right-wing bigots—quite rightly play no real part in our political debate. Where is our Sarah Vowell?

Ken Kalfus's *A Disorder Peculiar to the Country* made a wonderful accompaniment to Anthony's book. You've probably read it already, so you know that it's about the frighteningly unpleasant, horribly believable end of a marriage, set during and after 9/11. The book opens with both parties having reason to hope that the other might have been killed, either in the Twin Towers or on a plane, and if you haven't read it already, then you will know from my synopsis of this narrative fragment whether you have the stomach for the rest of the novel. If the book has caught you at just the right point in your relationship, you'll wolf it down. And just in case my wife bothers to read this: I'm not talking about us, darling. At the time I wrote these words we were getting on well. I wolfed it down for entirely literary reasons. *A Disorder Peculiar to the Country* is a sophisticated piece of adult entertainment (and by the way, that last word is never used pejoratively or patronizingly in these pages), full of mess and paranoia and an invigorating viciousness, and it takes narrative risks, too, a rare quality in a novel that is essentially naturalistic and uninterested in formal experiment. Not all of them come off, but when they do—and the vertiginous ending is one that does, in spades—you feel as though this is a fictional voice that you haven't heard before.

So the plate with the other half of the cake on it was, like, an art plate, and I have to say that I haven't eaten it all yet. I'm two-thirds of the way through Russo's *Bridge of Sighs* and about halfway through Weschler's Robert Irwin book, and my suspicion is that I won't finish the latter. I'm so confused about the house rules that I'm really not sure whether I'm allowed to say that or not, even though it's a simple statement of fact; harboring a suspicion that you won't finish a book is almost certainly a crime, and I'm almost certainly looking at a one-month suspension, but I don't care. My reluctance to finish the book has nothing to do with Lawrence Weschler; it's because I enjoyed *Everything That Rises,* his brilliant collection of essays, that I went out (or stayed in, anyway) and bought this one. It's more that the subject of his book is a minimalist artist, and when it comes to minimalist art, I am, I realize, an agnostic, maybe even an atheist.

I use these words because it seems to me that it's something you either believe in or you don't—a choice you're not really given with a Hockney or a Hopper or a Monet. Here's Irwin (clearly a likable, thoughtful man, incidentally) on his late line paintings, which consist of several straight lines on an orange background:

> When you look... at them perceptually, you find that your eye ends up suspended in midair, midspace or even midstride: time and space seem to blend in the continuum of your presence. You lose your bearings for a moment. You end up in a totally meditative state.

Well, what if that doesn't happen to you? I mean, it doesn't happen to everyone, right? What are you left with? And it occurred to me that Catholics could make a similar claim about what happens when you receive communion. There's a big difference between the body of Christ and a bit of wafer.

I shall write about Russo's absorbing, painstakingly detailed novel next month, when I've finished it. But I kept muddling up Irwin with Russo's artist character Noonan—not because the art they make is at all similar, but because the journeys they take both seem so unlikely. Noonan is a small-town no-hoper with a hateful father who grows up to be one of America's most celebrated painters; Irwin was a working-class kid from L.A. who loved cars and girls, went into the army, and then embarked on an extraordinary theoretical journey that ends with the blurring of the space-time continuum. When you read about the two lives simultaneously, one adds credibility to the other.

Louis Sachar's *Holes* is funny, gripping, and sad, a Boy's Own Adventure story rewritten by Kurt Vonnegut. Do you people ever do light reading, or is it all concrete poetry and state-of-the-nation novels? Because if you ever do take any time out, may I make a suggestion? These young-adult novels I've been Hoovering up are not light in the sense that they are disposable or unmemorable. On the contrary, they have all, without exception, been smart, complicated, deeply felt, deeply meant. They are light, however, in the sense that they are not built to resist your interest in them: they want to be read quickly and effortlessly. So instead of reading the ninth book in a detective series, why not knock off a modern classic instead?

P.S. Well, that didn't take long. I have been suspended for one issue. "Willful failure to finish a book," it says here, "thereby causing distress to a fellow author and failing in your duty to literature and/or criticism." Ho hum. This has happened so often that it's water off a duck's back. See you in a couple of months. ✷

JANUARY 2008

I have recently spent two weeks traveling around your country—if your country is the one with the crazy time zones and the constant television advertisements for erectile dysfunction cures—on a fact-finding mission for this magazine: the Polysyllabic Spree, the forty-seven literature-loving, unnervingly even-tempered yet unsmiling young men and women who remove all the good jokes from this column every month, came to the conclusion that I am no longer in touch with American reading habits, and sent me on an admittedly enlightening tour of airport bookshops. This is how I know that your favorite writer is not Cormac McCarthy, nor even David Foster Wallace, but someone called Joel Osteen, who may even be a member of the Spree, for all I know: he has the same perfect teeth, and the same belief in the perfectibility of man through the agency of Jesus Christ our savior. Osteen was on TV every time I turned it on—thank heaven for the adult pay-per-view channels!—and his book *Become a Better You* was everywhere. I suppose I'll have to read it now, if only to find out what you are all thinking.

True story: I saw one person, an attractive thirtysomething woman, actually buy the book, in the bookstore at the George Bush Intercontinental Airport in Houston, Texas, and, perhaps significantly, she was weeping as she did so. She ran in, tears streaming down her face and muttering to herself, and went straight to the nonfiction hardback bestsellers display. Your guess is as good as mine. I am almost certain that a feckless man was to blame (I suspect that she had been dumped somewhere between gates D15 and D17), and indeed, that feckless American men are generally responsible for the popularity of Christianity in the United States. In England, interestingly, the men are not in the least bit feckless, and, as a result, we are an almost entirely godless nation, and Joel Osteen is never on our televisions.

I wrote this last paragraph shortly before going to the gym, where for twenty minutes or so I wondered how to link the story of the weeping woman to Tom Perrotta's *The Abstinence Teacher;* I just couldn't see a smooth way of doing it. As *The Abstinence Teacher* is, in part, about a feckless American male's rebirth as a Christian, I ended my session on the cross-trainer wondering instead whether my tour of U.S. airport bookshops has left me brain-damaged. I am almost sure it do has.

I should say that I read a U.K. proof copy of *The Abstinence Teacher,* and that on the cover it claims that Tom Perrotta is an American... well, an American *me.* This is a high-risk, possibly even foolishly misguided marketing strategy, and does no justice to Perrotta's talent. And it says a lot about my admiration for him, and my interest in what he has to say on what puzzles those over here most about the U.S., that I overcame my initial dismay and wolfed it down, albeit with the spine cracked, so that I could carry it around inside-out. Needless to say, I end up absurdly flattered by the comparison: *The Abstinence Teacher* is a clever, funny, thoughtful, and sympathetic novel.

Perrotta's initial focus is on Ruth Ramsey, a sex-education teacher who is having trouble with her school governors and the local evangelical church after telling her students, with a careless neutrality, that some people enjoy oral sex. When her daughter's soccer coach, a member of the church, leads the team in impromptu prayer after a victory, her outrage and grievance lure her into a confrontation that provides the bulk of the narrative. What is particularly daring about *The Abstinence Teacher,* given Perrotta's constituency, is that he isn't afraid to switch point of view: it's all very well, and for Perrotta (I'm guessing) not particularly difficult, to give us access to the mind of a liberal sex-education teacher, but attempting to raise sympathy for a formerly deadbeat born-again is another matter. Perrotta's Tim is a triumphant creation, believable and human. It helps that he's a burned-out ex-musician who's turned to the Lord to help him through his various dependencies—there but for the grace of God go the readers and writers of this magazine, and certainly half the potential readership of a literary novel. And Tim's nagging doubt is attractive, too. Where Perrotta really scores, though, is in his detailed imagining of his character's journey. It seems entirely credible, for example, that Tim should have a particular problem with Christian sex: he knows that the drugs and the alcohol were harmful, and are therefore best avoided. But seeing as he has to have sex anyway, with his naïve and subservient Christian second wife, he cannot help but feel nostalgic for the old-school, hot and godless variety. I'm betting that this is exactly how it is for those who have followed Tim's path to redemption.

There was a similar collision between Christianity and liberalism in the canceled TV series *Studio 60 on the Sunset Strip,* but it didn't make much of a noise, mostly because the Christian character, or, rather, her determination to appear on a satirical liberal entertainment program weekly, constantly stretched our credulity until our credulity tore right down the middle. Perrotta, on the other hand, employs his considerable skill to ensure that Tim and Ruth are an accident waiting to happen.

Just recently, I read an interview with a contemporary literary novelist who worried that books by other writers who use pop-culture references in their fiction would not be read in twenty-five years' time. And, yes, there's a possibility that in a quarter of a century, *The Abstinence Teacher* will mystify people who come across it: it's about America today, this minute, and it's chock-full of band names and movies and TV programs. (One or two passages may mystify people who live in soccer-playing nations now, but I enjoyed the book too much to take issue with Perrotta about his failure to grasp the insignificance of the throw-in.) Yet some fiction at least should deal with the state of the here and now, no matter what the cost to the work's durability, no? This novel takes on an important subject—namely, the clash between two currently prevailing cultures opposed to an almost ludicrous degree—that is in urgent need of consideration by a writer as smart and as humane as Tom Perrotta. My advice to you: don't read writers with an eye on posterity. They are deeply serious people, and by picking up their books now, you are trivializing them. Plus, they're not interested in the money. They're above all that.

I have been writing this column for so long that I am now forced to consider a novel by my brother-in-law *for the third time.* Irritatingly, it's just as good as the other two, although it's a lot less Roman than either *Pompeii* or *Imperium,* which may or may not show some encouraging signs of failure and/or weakness. In fact, *The Ghost* is Robert's first novel set in the present day, and, like *The Abstinence Teacher,* you don't want to wait twenty-five years to read it: it's about the relationship between Adam Lang, an ex–prime minister whose bafflingly close relationship with the U.S.A. has cost him a great deal, and his ghostwriter, whose research uncovers things that Lang would prefer remain covered up. As the two of them work together in a wintry Martha's Vineyard, Lang's world starts to fall apart. *The Ghost* is one part thriller, one part political commentary, and one part the angry wish-fulfillment of an enraged liberal, and it has enough narrative energy to fuel a Combat Shadow. It also has a very neat GPS scene in it, the first I've come across in contemporary fiction. It has been said that Tony Blair is extremely vexed by *The Ghost,* so you don't even have to read it to feel its beneficent effects. If that's not a definition of great literature, then I don't know what is.

The last time I was here, I promised to return to Richard Russo's *Bridge of Sighs,* which I hadn't quite finished. Well, I finished it, and liked it (although not as much as I liked *Empire Falls,* which is an all-time favorite), and no longer feel competent to write about it. I started it on a sun-lounger in France, and it's now November, and Lou "Lucy" Lynch and his careful, gentle ruminations seem a lifetime ago. The same goes for Paul Zindel's *The Pigman,* this month's YA experience—I know I read it, but I'm not entirely sure I could tell you an awful lot about it. Maybe I should have done my book report the moment I finished it.

I recently discovered that when my friend Mary has finished a book, she won't start another for a couple of days—she wants to give her most recent reading experience a little more time to breathe, before it's suffocated by the next. This makes sense, and it's an entirely laudable policy, I think. Those of us who read neurotically, however—to ward off boredom, and the fear of our own ignorance, and our impending deaths—can't afford the time.

Speaking of which… Jeff Gordinier's forthcoming *X Saves the World* (subtitled *How Generation X Got the Shaft but Can Still Keep Everything from Sucking*) begins with an apposite quote from

Douglas Coupland's novel *Generation X:* "My life had become a series of scary incidents that simply weren't stringing together to make for an interesting book, and God, you get old so quickly! Time was (and is) running out." *X Saves the World* starts with the assumption that the Boomers (born in the late '40s and '50s) have all sold out, and the Millennials are all nightmarish Britney clones who can't go to the toilet without filming the experience in anticipation of an MTV reality show. And that leaves Generation X, a.k.a. the slackers, a.k.a. the postmodern ironists, a.k.a. blah blah, to make something of the sorry mess we call, like, "the world." Gordinier, of course, is neither a Boomer nor a Millennial, which might in some eyes make his generalizations even more suspect than generalizations usually are, but I loved this book anyway: it's impassioned, very quick on its feet, dense with all the right allusions—Kurt Cobain, the Replacements, Susan Sontag, Henry James, and the rest of that whole crowd—funny, and, in the end, actually rather moving.

And it's convincing, too, although of course it's hard to talk about generational mores and attitudes without raising all the old questions about when generations begin and end, and how we as a collection of individuals, as opposed to a banner-waving mob, are supposed to fit into it all neatly. As far as I can tell, I'm supposed to be a Boomer, but I was twelve when Woodstock took place, nineteen when *Anarchy in the U.K.* was released, and always felt closer to Johnny Rotten and everything that came after than to David Crosby, so where am I supposed to fit into all this? There were Boomers that never sold out, plenty of Xers that did, and lots of lovable Millennials who worry about global warming and literacy levels. There have always been relentless and empty-headed self-promoters, although in the good old days we used to ignore them, rather than give them their own reality show. Gordinier is right, though, I think, when he argues that Generation X (and I know that even naming you like this makes me sound cheesy and square, but I can't say "so-called" every time, nor can I raise my eyebrows and roll my eyes in print) has found another way of doing things, and that this way may well add up to something significant. This is a generation that not only understands technology but has internalized its capabilities, thus enabling it to think in a different way; this is a generation that knows that it can't change the world, a recognition that enables it to do what it can. Cinema, books, TV, and music have all produced something new as a result, so long as you know where to look.

I suspect that those who write about Gordinier's book will engage him in his argument, and that very few people will point out how much fun this book is to read, but it is; the last chapter, which uses Henry James's novella *The Beast in the Jungle* and the life and work of James Brown as the ingredients for a passionate rallying cry, is particularly fizzy.

In other news: nearly a third of the football season is over, and Arsenal, still undefeated, is sitting at the top of the Premier League, despite having sold Thierry Henry to Barcelona in the summer. These are golden days, my friends, for another couple of weeks at least. This is how to become a better you: choose Arsène Wenger, Arsenal's brilliant manager, as your life coach. I did, and look at me now. If I found myself weeping in an airport, that's the book I'd buy: *Think Offensively, the Arsène Wenger Way,* but he hasn't written it yet. (You'll be reading about it here first if he ever does.) Mind you, even Joel Osteen would be able to see that we need a new goalkeeper urgently. ✶

FEBRUARY 2008

BOOKS BOUGHT:
* *The Raymond Chandler Papers: Selected Letters and Nonfiction 1909–1959*

BOOKS READ:
* *What Sport Tells Us About Life*—Ed Smith
* *The Absolutely True Diary of a Part-Time Indian*— Sherman Alexie
* *The Darling*— Russell Banks
* *The Rights of the Reader*—Daniel Pennac

The best description I know of what it feels like to learn to read comes in Francis Spufford's brilliant memoir *The Child That Books Built:*

When I caught the mumps, I couldn't read; when I went back to school again, I could. The first page of *The Hobbit* was a thicket of symbols, to be decoded one at a time and joined hesitantly together....By the time I reached *The Hobbit*'s last page, though, writing had softened, and lost the outlines of the printed alphabet, and become a transparent liquid, first viscous and sluggish, like a jelly of meaning, then ever thinner and more mobile, flowing faster and faster, until it reached me at the speed of thinking and I could not entirely distinguish the suggestions it was making from my own thoughts. I had undergone the acceleration into the written word that you also experience as a change in the medium. In fact, writing had ceased to be a thing—an object in the world—and *become* a medium, a substance you look through.

Firstly, we should note that the first book Spufford ever read was *The Hobbit,* a book that I still haven't picked up, partly because I am afraid I still won't understand it. Secondly, Spufford caught the mumps just as he turned six—he is one of the cleverest people I have ever come across, and yet some parents with young children would be freaking out if their kids weren't able to read by then. And lastly, I would just like to point out that you can't fake a memory like this. Learning to read happens once and once only for most of us, and for the vast majority of adults in first-world countries it happened a long time ago. You have to dig deep, deep down into the bog of the almost lost, and then carry what you have found carefully to the surface, and then you have to find the words and images to describe what you see on your spade. Perhaps Spufford's amazing feat of recollection means nothing to you; but when I first read it, I knew absolutely that this was what happened to me. I too spooned up the jelly of meaning.

I turned back to Spufford's book because my five-year-old is on the verge of reading. (Yeah, you read that right, Spufford. Five! And only just! Francis Spufford was born in 1964 and this book was published in 2003, so by my reckoning my son will have produced something as good as *The Child That Books Built* by the year 2040, or something slightly better by 2041.) Writing hasn't softened for him: three-letter words are as insoluble as granite, and he can no more look through writing than he can look through his bedroom wall. The good news is that he's almost frenetically motivated; the bad news is that he is so eager to learn because he has got it into his head that he will be given a Nintendo DS machine when he can read and write, which he argues that he can do now to his own satisfaction—he can write his own name, and read the words *Mum, Dad, Spider, Man,* and at least eight others. As far as he is concerned, literacy is something that he can dispense with altogether in a couple of months, when the Nintendo turns up. It will have served its purpose.

Daniel Pennac's *The Rights of the Reader,* first published sixteen years ago in France, the author's native country, is a really rather lovely book about all the things parents and teachers do to discourage the art and habit of reading, and all the things we could do to persuade young people that literacy is worth keeping about one's person even after you've got it nailed. According to Pennac, we have spent most of our five-year-old son's life teaching him that reading is something to be endured: we threaten to withdraw stories at bedtime, and then never follow through with the threat ("an unbearable punishment, for them and for us," Pennac points out, and this is just one of the many moments of wisdom that will make you want him to be your adoptive dad); we dangle television and computers as rewards; we occasionally try to force him to read when he is demotivated, tired, bolshy. ("The lightness of our sentences stopped them getting bogged down: now having to mumble indecipherable letters stifles even their ability to dream," says Pennac sadly.) All of these mistakes, it seems to me, are unavoidable at some time in the average parenting week, although Pennac does us a favor by exposing the perverse logic buried in them.

What's great about *The Rights of the Reader* is Pennac's tone—by turns wry, sad, amused, hopeful—and his endless fund of good sense: he likes his canon, but doesn't want to torture you into reading it, and rights 2 and 3 (the Right to Skip and the Right Not to Finish a Book) are, we must remind ourselves, fundamental human rights. The French book about reading that's been getting a lot of attention recently is Pierre Bayard's *How to Talk About Books You*

Haven't Read, which should surely be retitled *You Need Some New Friends, Because the Ones You've Got Are Jerks:* literary editors seem to think it's zeitgeisty, but out in the world, grown-ups no longer feel the need to bullshit about literature, thank god. Pennac's book is the one we should all be thinking about, because its author hasn't given up. *The Rights of the Reader* is full of great quotes, too. Here's one of my favorites, from Flannery O'Connor: "If teachers are in the habit of approaching a story as if it were a research problem for which any answer is believable so long as it is not obvious, then I think students will never learn to enjoy fiction." That one is dedicated to anyone who graduated from college and found themselves unable to read anything that came from the imagination.

Russell Banks's *The Darling* was recommended to me—*given* to me, even—by the owner of a wonderful independent bookstore, Rakestraw Books, in Danville, California; booksellers know better than anyone that talking about books you have read is much more persuasive than attempting to sound smart about books you haven't. It's the second great novel about Africa by an American writer that I've read in the last year (I'm forbidden from talking about the other one by internal bureaucracy), although the creative impulse behind Banks's book is much tougher to read. It's in some ways a peculiar novel, in that it tracks the journey of a 1960s radical, the daughter of a famous pediatrician, as she travels all the way from the Weather Underground to war-torn Liberia, where she marries a local politician and takes care of chimpanzees. A crude synopsis is only likely to provoke the question "What the *fuck?*" but then, synopses are rarely much use when it comes to novels. Whatever prompted Banks to write *The Darling,* the material here provides him with an enormous and dazzling armory of ironies and echoes, and his narrator, Hannah, by turns passionately engaged and icily detached, is inevitably reminiscent of a Graham Greene character. This is a novel that provides a potted history of Liberia, a dreamy, extended meditation on the connections between humans and apes, a convincing examination of the internal life of an American refusenik, and an acute portrait of a mixed-race, cross-cultural marriage, and if you're not interested in any of that, then we at the *Believer* politely suggest that you'd be happier with another magazine.

I nearly didn't read Sherman Alexie's *The Absolutely True Diary of a Part-Time Indian,* because I had decided that, as we had both had young-adult novels published at around the same time, we were somehow in competition, and that his book was the Yankees, or Manchester United, or Australia, or any other sporting nemesis you care to name. And of course hearing that Alexie's novel was great really didn't help overcome my reluctance—rather, it merely hardened it. I'd like to think that by reading the book I have demonstrated some kind of maturity, and come to recognize that books are not like sports teams and therefore can't play each other; mine can't advance to the next round by dint of all-around physical superiority, no matter how thoroughly I coach it, no matter what diet I put it on, no matter how many steroids I force down its little throat. (If I thought that giving my novel performance-enhancing drugs would help it in any way, I'd do it, though, and I'm not ashamed to admit it.)

Anyway, *The Absolutely True Diary of a Part-Time Indian* is, as I was told on my recent book tour by scores of unsupportive and thoughtless people, a terrific book, funny and moving and effortlessly engaging. The part-time Indian of the title is Junior, a hydrocephalic weakling whose decision to enroll at the white high school at the edge of his reservation costs him both his closest friendship and respect from his community; it's a coming-of-age story, but it's fresh: I for one knew nothing about the world that Alexie describes, and in any case Junior's defiant, worldly-wise, sad, scared voice, and Ellen Forney's cute and sympathetic drawings give the book the feeling of a modern YA classic. And, seeing as the best YA fiction (see previous columns) is as punchy and engaging as anything you might come across in a bookstore, it's for you, too. If you see Sherman Alexie's novel getting a beating some-where—in the ring, at a racetrack, or anywhere else you're likely to see books competing—then demand a urine test, because some-body's cheating.

I have written about Ed Smith before: his last book, *On and Off the Field,* was a diary of his season, and as he's a cricketer, I pre-sumed that my banging on about a sport you didn't know, under-stand, or care about would annoy you, in a satisfying way. It's great, then, that he has another book coming out, this time a collection of essays dealing with the areas where sport (quite often cricket) is able to shed light on other areas of life. In the first essay he ex-plains why there will never be another Don Bradman, but as you lot don't even know that you've missed the first Bradman alto-gether, it's a waste of time and column inches going into any fur-ther detail, so that's what I'll do. Bradman's batting average, the *New York Times* concluded in its 2001 obituary after some fancy mathematics, meant that he was better than Michael Jordan, Babe Ruth, and Ty Cobb; nobody has got anywhere close to his record since, just as in baseball nobody has managed a .400 season since Ted Williams in 1941. (We weren't playing professional sports in 1941, you know. We were too busy fighting Nazis—an old griev-ance, maybe, but not one that anyone here is likely to forget for another few hundred years.) Smith argues that the increasing pro-fessionalism of sports means that it's much harder for sporting gi-ants to tower quite as high over their peers: greater defensive com-petence and organization have resulted in a bunching somewhere nearer the middle. The bad players and teams are much better than they used to be, which means that the good ones find it harder to exert their superiority so crushingly. And when it comes to ath-letics, we can't get much faster, according to a Harvard evolution-ary geneticist—"the laws of oxygen exchange will not permit it." Did you know that horses have stopped breaking racing records?

They've now been bred to the point where they simply can't get any faster. I could eat this stuff up with a spoon.

You'll enjoy this: when the cricketer Fred Titmus made his professional debut, the tannoy announcer felt obliged to correct an error on the score card: "F. J. Titmus should, of course, read Titmus, F. J." An amateur player (a "gentleman," in the class-bound language of cricket) was allowed to put his initials before his surname; a player—in other words, a professional—had to put his initials after. Titmus was being put in his place—in *1949*. What a stupid country. This is why I have repeatedly turned down a knighthood. Knighthoods are no good to anyone, if they want to get on in Britain. I'm holding out for a lordship.

The chapter on what we can learn from amateurism (a word which, it's easy to forget, has its roots in the old-school, first-lesson *amo amas amat*) is of value to pretty much any of us who have managed to end up doing what we love for a living. Anyone in this privileged position who has never for a moment experienced self-consciousness, or endured a bout of second-guessing, or ended up wondering what it was they loved in the first place is either mad or isn't getting paid a living wage (and now I come to think about it, pretty much every writer I have ever met belongs in one of these two camps). Smith's entertaining exploration of creativity and inspiration would be every bit as useful to a poet or a songwriter (and he ropes in Dylan to help make his case) as it would be to an opening batsman. Ha! So you might actually have to read this book about cricket! Even better!

Next month, apparently, this column will be titled "Stuff I've Been Watching" (for one issue only). I only watch *30 Rock* and *Match of the Day*. I'd skip it, if I were you, unless you want to know whether Lee Dixon is a better postmatch pundit than Alan Shearer. Actually, I'll tell you now, and save you the trouble: he is. Defenders are always better analysts than forwards. In this, as in so many other areas, sport is exactly like life. ✷

MARCH/APRIL 2008

At first I was afraid. In fact, I was, indeed, petrified. "Stuff I've Been Watching"? Are they sure? Even… this? And *that*? And if I own up, will they still let me write about stuff I've been reading? Or will the stuff I've watched count against me, on the grounds that anyone who watches either this or that is highly unlikely to know which way up you hold a book? I should admit straightaway that "this" and "that" contain no pornographic content whatsoever. "This" is likely to be, in any given month, a football match between two village teams battling for a chance to play in the first qualifying round of the FA Cup; "that," on the other hand, could very well be a repeat of a 1990s quiz show—

Family Fortunes, say—broadcast on one of the U.K.'s many excellent quiz-show rerun channels. This isn't all I watch, of course. There are the endless games between proper football teams, and the first-run quiz shows, but I'm not embarrassed about watching them. Like many parents, I go to the cinema rarely, because going to the cinema means going without dinner, and no film is worth that, really, with the possible exception of *Citizen Kane,* and I saw that on TV.

As luck would have it, however, I have been asked to write about stuff I watched in December, and in December I watch screener copies of movies on DVD. I am a member of BAFTA, the British Academy of Film and Television Arts, which means that at the end of the year, every half-decent film that might have half a chance of winning an award is pushed through my letterbox. For free. The DVDs are piled high on a shelf in my living room, new films by Ang Lee and Paul Thomas Anderson, adaptations of books by Ian McEwan and Monica Ali, and they look… You know what? They look pretty daunting. Stacked up like that, they look not unlike books, in fact: already some of them are starting to give off the same slightly musty, worthy smell that you don't really want to associate with the cinema. Every year, some of them—many of them— will go unwatched. We're getting through a few of them, though. (And please welcome the first-person-plural pronoun to this column. Books are "I," but movies are "we," because that's how they get watched. Any views expressed herein, however, are mine, unless I manage to offend somebody in Hollywood with power and wealth, in which case that particular view was hers. She won't care. She's only an independent film producer.) So, from the top…

Just before Christmas, I was browsing the biography section of a chain bookstore, hopelessly looking for presents, when, suddenly and bewilderingly, the color drained out of the book jackets: they had all turned sepia or white. I was almost certain that I'd been stricken by a rare medical condition until I realized that I had reached the section reserved for the genre known in the U.K. as the "misery memoir." These books, all inspired by the enormous success of Dave Pelzer, seem to deal exclusively with childhood hardship and abuse, and have titles like *Please Daddy, Put It Away;* the jackets are white or sepia, apart from a washed-out photo, because Pelzer's books look like that. Anyway, in this chain bookstore, these memoirs had all been bunched together in a section called "Real Lives"—as if Churchill or Katharine Hepburn or Tobias Wolff or Mary Karr had lived unreal lives.

I was reminded of the Real Lives section when I was watching *This Is England,* a British independent film by the talented young English director Shane Meadows: there is a similarly hubristic claim to authenticity in the movie's title. Is the country depicted really England? Like, the whole of it? I've lived in England all my life, but I didn't recognize Meadows's version. He'd say that this is because I've spent my time in the soft south of the country, and he's made a film about the gritty north, and that's fair enough, although I'd be resistant to any argument that his England is more real than mine. What concerned me more is that some of the details on which any claim to authenticity must rest felt a little off to me. Why did the characters all have different regional accents, when the film is set in one depressed suburb of a northern English city? Were young no-hoper English skinheads really listening to Toots and the Maytals in 1983, or would they have stuck to their Madness and Bad Manners records? And did they really have instant access to the mythology of Woodstock when they were teasing their peers about clothes and haircuts? *This Is England* is a semi-autobiographical film about a twelve-year-old falling in with a dodgy crowd around the time of the Falklands War, when Margaret Thatcher's repulsive jingo-ism got roughly translated by some disenfranchised working-class kids into the violent and racist language of the far Right. It's never less than gripping, not least because Meadows gets exemplary performances from all his actors, especially thirteen-year-old Thomas

Turgoose as Shaun. Any film that ends with the one black character being kicked half to death by a psychotic skinhead is always going to be hard to adore, but I'm glad I watched it.

We watched... Actually, I'd better just check something. Hey,
Spree! Do the same rules apply to movies as to books? We still
have to be nice? Or say nothing at all? Yes? OK. So, we watched
a film directed by a famous director and starring famous people,
and—as film agents say—we didn't love it. (Top tip: if a film agent
ever tells you that he or she didn't love your novel or script, then
you might as well kill yourself, because you're dead anyway.) This
particular film was about unpleasant people doing unkind things
for increasingly contrived reasons, and though that's pretty much
the dominant Hollywood genre, this one felt particularly phony. It
was gloomy and portentous, too, which is presumably why it's being pushed through letterboxes during the awards season.

I did, however, love Todd Haynes's clever, thoughtful, frequently
dazzling meditation on the subject of Bob Dylan, *I'm Not There,*
which, as you must surely know by now, stars Cate Blanchett as
one of six actors taking on Dylan's various incarnations and perso-
nas. If you'd decided not to see it because it sounded gimmicky or
just plain daft, then you should think again: I can't guarantee that
you'll like it, obviously, but I'm positive that you won't dislike it on
the grounds that Cate Blanchett and a fourteen-year-old black kid
called Marcus Carl Franklin are being asked to interpret the career
of someone who doesn't resemble them physically. On the contrary, one of the film's many triumphs is that you never question
it for a second—or rather, any questioning you do is on the filmmakers' own terms and at their behest, and as a consequence this
helps you to engage with the endless complexity of both the material and Dylan himself.

None of these characters is called "Bob Dylan." Blanchett is
Jude, the electric speed-freak *Don't Look Back*–era Bob (and her
sections are occasionally reminiscent of D. A. Pennebaker's shaky

handheld documentary, when they're not borrowing from Richard Lester or *Blowup*); the character's name is suitably androgynous, and of course contains an echo of that famous 1966 taunt, which comes in handy when the moment arrives. Franklin plays a folksinger called Woody, who rides trains with hobos and carries around a guitar case bearing the familiar legend THIS MACHINE KILLS FASCISTS. "It's 1959 and he's singing about boxcars?" a kindly woman who has taken Woody in and fed him asks witheringly, right at the start of the picture. "Live your own time, child. Sing your own time." This is a pretty good example of how Haynes has externalized and dramatized all the internal conversations Dylan must have had with himself over the last fifty-odd years, but it also provides the quest for all the characters: what and where is one's own time? Richard Gere's Billy the Kid is lost in a Pat Garrett/Lily, Rosemary Old West full of robber barons and the disenfranchised poor, and Jude, the most "modern" of any of the versions available, ends up running back into his/her own head. Meanwhile, Heath Ledger's Robbie, living in the here and now, splits painfully, *Blood on the Tracks* style, from Charlotte Gainsbourg. So what use is the here and now, if all it can do is break your heart? Haynes has enormous fun with, and finds great profit in, the iconography of Dylan. There's so much of it that even a casual shot of a young couple huddled together against the cold, or a jokey montage scene showing Ledger bashing into a couple of dustbins while learning to ride a motorbike, teems with meaning. It's the best film about an artist that I've ever seen: it's meltingly beautiful and it has taken the trouble to engage its subject with love, care, and intelligence. What more do you want? Even if you hate every decision that Haynes has made, you can enjoy it as the best feature-length pop video ever made. Who wouldn't want to watch Heath Ledger and Charlotte Gainsbourg making love while "I Want You" plays on the sound track?

There were two visits to cinemas this month, a family outing to see *The Simpsons Movie,* and a rare adults-only evening out for *Juno.* I can tell you little about *The Simpsons Movie* because—and I'm not big enough to resist naming names—Mila Douglas, five-year-old best friend of my middle son, was scared of it, and as her parents weren't with her, it was me that had to keep taking her out into the foyer, where she made a miraculous and immediate recovery every time. Scared! Of the Simpsons! I will cheerfully admit that I have failed as a father in pretty much every way bar one: my boys have been trained ruthlessly to watch whatever I make them watch. They won't flinch for a second, no matter who is being disemboweled on the screen in front of them. Mila (who is, perhaps not coincidentally, a girl) has, by contrast, clearly been "well brought up," by parents who "care," and who probably "think" about what is "age-appropriate." Yeah, well. What good did that do her on an afternoon excursion with the Hornby family? From what I saw, the movie was as good as, but no better than, three average *Simpsons* episodes bolted together—an average *Simpsons* episode being, of course, smarter than an average Flaubert novel. It could well be, though, that I was sitting in the foyer listening to Mila Douglas's views on birthday-party fashion etiquette during the best jokes.

By the time you read this, there's probably a *Juno* backlash going on, and smart people are describing it as too cute and kooky for its own good. Well, I'm stuck in 2007, and in 2007 we still think that *Juno* is charming and funny and that Michael Cera is a comic genius. *Juno* also features the first but almost certainly not the last cinematic reference to a quarterly magazine based not too far from Believer Towers. We at the *Believer* are used to being talked about in the movies—there was a surprisingly well-informed conversation about our decision to take advertising in *Live Free or Die Hard,* and an affectionate spoof of the Spree in *Alvin and the Chipmunks.* It's about time our poor relations caught up.

I'm in the middle of watching *And When Did You Last See Your Father?* as we speak—I stopped last night just when I got to the bit about fecal vomit, but I'll watch Jim Broadbent die of bowel cancer this evening, if my morale is high enough. This movie was produced by a friend, directed by another friend, and stars a third. It was adapted by a neighbor from a memoir written by a guy I see from time to time and whose book I admired very much. What do I think of it so far? I think it's brilliantly produced, directed, acted, and written, and the source material is fantastic. Also, it's really good. ✶

MAY 2008

L ast month, I wrote about stuff I'd been watching, and while I was writing about stuff I'd been watching, I was thinking about the stuff I wasn't reading. I wasn't not reading because of the watching; I was simply not reading. Or rather, I was simply not reading complete books. I tried, several times; I began Martin Gayford's *The Yellow House*, about the nine weeks that Gauguin and van Gogh spent as roommates, and Matt Ridley's *Genome*, and Dickens's *Barnaby Rudge*, and Meg Wolitzer's *The Position*, and Irmgard Keun's *Child of All Nations*, and Roberto Saviano's *Gomorrah: Italy's Other Mafia*, and John Mullan's *Anonymity*, and I read a couple of entries in

Clive James's *Cultural Amnesia,* and nothing took. None of this, of course, is the fault of these fine authors or their almost certainly brilliant work. I was just itchy and scratchy and probably crusty, too, and I began to wonder whether I had simply lost the habit—the skill, even—of reading. I was beginning to feel that this one long, pained explanation would have to serve as my last in this space, which I would then simply hand over to someone young enough to plow all the way through to the end, or at least the middle, of anything they start. (Although isn't that supposed to be one of the problems with young people? That their brains have been so rotted by Internet pornography and Nintendo that they are physically incapable of reading anything longer than a cereal packet? Maybe I will prove impossible to replace, and as long as I read a few opening paragraphs every month, this gig is mine forever.) At least I have some facts at my disposal. Did you know that if you wrote out the human genome, one letter per millimeter, the text would be as long as the river Danube? Did you know that the most expensive living artist in 1876 was Meissonier, one of whose paintings went for nearly four hundred thousand francs? These are two of the many things I've learned by reading the beginnings of this month's books. I am beginning to think that this new regime will be ideal for my dotage. I can read the beginnings of a few books, sit at the bar at my local, and regale people with fascinating nuggets of information. How can I fail to make friends if I know how long the human genome is?

Just as I was beginning to despair—and let's face it, a man who is tired of books is looking at an awful lot of *Rockford Files* reruns—a book lying on a trestle table in a local bookshop managed to communicate to me its desire to be read in its entirety, and I bought it, and I swallowed it whole. Quite why Graham Mc-Cann's *Spike & Co.,* about British comedy writing in the 1950s, should have succeeded in its siren call where scores of others failed remains mysterious. I had absolutely no previous desire to read it—I didn't even know it existed before the morning I bought it—and though I love a couple of the writers McCann discusses, I hadn't thought about them in a long while. Maybe the book nutritionists are right (and I'm sure that those of you who live in California probably have book nutritionists working for you full-time, maybe even living in your ubiquitous "guesthouses"): you need to listen to what your soul needs.

Spike & Co. is about a group of writers who formed a company called Associated London Scripts (they wanted to call themselves Associated British Scripts, but the local council turned them down on the grounds that they weren't big enough) who operated out of offices above a greengrocer's in Shepherd's Bush, and went on to change the course of British and American TV and radio writing. Out of these offices came *The Goon Show,* John Lennon's favorite radio show and a direct inspiration for Monty Python; *Steptoe and Son,* which became *Sanford and Son* in the U.S.; *'Til Death Us Do Part* (known to you lot as *All in the Family*); and the sci-fi series *Doctor Who,* which is still running, in an admittedly snazzier form, today. I have known and loved these shows for much of my life, and yet I had no idea about the greengrocer aspect of it all, which seems to me extraordinary. Two of my favorite writers—and I'm not talking about writers of TV and radio comedy, but writers of all denominations—Ray Galton and Alan Simpson, met in a TB sanatorium, and I didn't know that, either. They were both desperately ill teenagers, neither expected to live much into his twenties; they met toward the end of their stay in the late 1940s, and by the mid-'60s had produced *Hancock's Half Hour* and *Steptoe and Son,* two series that helped form the psyche of contemporary Britain. The chapter on Spike Milligan, meanwhile, provides an invaluable writing tip. "Once he had started work on a script he disliked ever having to stop; he wrote as he thought, and if he came to a place where the right line failed to emerge, he would just jab a finger at one of the keys, type 'FUCK IT' or 'BOLLOCKS,' and then carry on regardless. The first draft would feature plenty of such expletives, but then, with each successive version, the expletives grew fewer and fewer, until by about the tenth draft, he had a complete, expletive-free script." I have found this more helpful than I am prepared to talk about in any great depth, possibly because I can build my own inadequacies right into the page, rather than let them hover around the edges.

I can't hope or imagine that you'll enjoy this book as much as I did. Much of it will be incomprehensible to you, and in any case, you're not me. John Carey points out in his book *What Good Are the Arts?* that there are millions of tiny decisions and influences, over the course of a lifetime, that help us form our relationships with books and music and the rest of it, and if you and I shared even half a dozen of them, I'd be surprised. Even if you'd bought the book at the same time at the same store, you couldn't have spent the previous hour on my analyst's couch—I would have noticed, because I'd have been lying on top of you. But as a direct result of *Spike & Co.*, two things happened: (1) I bought a signed commemorative Galton and Simpson print off the Internet, and (2) I emailed a friend and asked him if he wanted to have a go at writing something with me, even though neither of us has TB or indeed any life-threatening infectious disease. *Spike & Co.* is a hymn to the joys of collaboration, and I suddenly became dissatisfied with the solitary nature of my day job. Such is the way of these things that nothing will come of it, of course, but we're having fun, and it's not often that you can say that about a day spent at a computer.

I read *The Shadow Catcher* and Junot Díaz's *The Brief Wondrous Life of Oscar Wao* because I had to: I agreed to judge the *Morning News*'s Rooster competition, in which the best books of last year are drawn against each other in a knockout competition. At the time of writing, there is no overall winner, but I can tell you that Díaz unsportingly thumped Wiggins in my round. He's twenty years younger and, as far as one can tell from the jacket photos, a lot tougher than Wiggins, but he didn't let any of that stop him. I hope he's ashamed of himself. His book, incidentally, is brilliant.

The reading hiatus came during and after all the film watching, but luckily for you, I read a couple of books before it, so you can't leave just yet. Alec Wilkinson's *The Happiest Man in the World* is a study of Poppa Neutrino, and the book's title worked on me just as it was supposed to: I wanted to know his secret. I was once sent a self-help book called *Should You Leave?* which was kicking around the house, in the way that books sometimes do, for months. Visitors would look at it, smile, pick it up, put it down, and then eventually start flicking through it. Nobody actually asked which page contained the answer, but you could see that they were hoping to stumble upon it without looking as though they were trying. It strikes me that anyone caught reading *The Happiest Man in the World* is owning up to a similar sort of dissatisfaction. I'm not sure, though, that Poppa Neutrino, a kind of Zen hobo who has spent his life rafting across the Atlantic, inventing new football plays, etc., can provide the answers we might be looking for. "He has begun to bleed constantly from his backside, so there is always a dark stripe down his pants...." "The box was six feet long, four feet tall and four feet wide.... He came and went from the box only when no one was around, because he didn't want anyone to know he was living in it." I was unable to put myself in Neutrino's position and imagine myself as anything other than thoroughly miserable, so I quickly gave up on the idea of discovering the route to my future happiness and looked instead for the source of his. This, too, remains elusive—indeed, Poppa Neutrino seems to spend so much time starving, having heart attacks, living in boxes, and bleeding from his backside that you can't help wondering whether there was a terrible mix-up, and whether the text belonging to this particular title is inside the cover of an altogether less-promising-looking book. And there is a sleight of hand played here, too. The reason that many of us cannot live a life free of grinding obligation is because we have mortgages, children, parents, friends, and so on. Presumably the mortgage payments on boxes are not onerous, but Neutrino certainly has children, few of whom are mentioned at any great length; this raises the suspicion that it's easier to avoid grinding obligation if one simply chooses to ignore it. Those who read the *New Yorker* will know that Alec Wilkinson is incapable of writing anything dull, or inelegant, and his obvious fascination with the subject gives the book a winning energy. That fascination, however, is not always entirely comprehensible.

The Happiest Man in the World made me think, though. Mostly I ended up thinking about the nature and value of experiences and memories, although I didn't get very far. Crossing the Atlantic on a raft or staying in to watch TV—it's all the same, in the end, isn't it? There comes a time when it's over, and all you can do is talk about it. And if that's the case, then… I'm sorry. If you bother with this column at all, it's probably because you're looking for book tips. You probably don't want to hear that all human endeavor is pointless.

Here's a tip: M. T. Anderson's *Feed*. This is yet another book that can be added to an increasingly long list titled "YA Novels I'd Never Heard of but Which Turn Out to Be Modern Classics," and *Feed* may well be the best of the lot. It's a sci-fi novel about a world in which everybody is plugged directly into a never-ending stream of text messages, shopping recommendations, pop music, and movie trailers—this is metaphor rather than prediction—and as a consequence Anderson's characters are frighteningly malleable and disturbingly inarticulate. Even the president of the U.S. has trouble with words! *Feed* is funny, serious, sad (there's a heartbreaking doomed romance at the center), and superbly realized; the moment I finished it I bought Anderson's latest novel, which is completely different. It's set in 1775, and it's about a boy who's raised by a group of rational philosophers, so it sounds like the author has allowed himself to be seduced by the promise of a quick buck.

I haven't even read the beginning of it yet, though. It's a novel, so I very much doubt whether there will be any interesting facts in the opening pages. I rather fear that I'm turning into my father. ✶

SEPTEMBER 2008

BOOKS BOUGHT:

* *Pictures at a Revolution*—
  Mark Harris
* *The Pumpkin Eater*—
  Penelope Mortimer
* *Daddy's Gone a' Huntin'*—
  Penelope Mortimer
* *The Last Campaign*—
  Thurston Clarke
* *Lush Life*—Richard Price
* *The Greek Way*—
  Edith Hamilton
* *Nixonland*—Rick Perlstein
* *Netherland*—Joseph O'Neill

BOOKS READ:

* *Pictures at a Revolution*—
  Mark Harris
* *The Pumpkin Eater*—
  Penelope Mortimer
* *Lush Life*—Richard Price
* *The Last Campaign*—
  Thurston Clarke
* *Cary Grant*—Graham
  McCann

If you were given a month to learn something about a subject about which you had hitherto known nothing, what would you choose? Quantum physics, maybe, or the works of Willa Cather, or the Hundred Years War? Would you learn a language, or possibly teach yourself how to administer first aid in the event of a domestic accident? I only ask because in the last month I have read everything there is to read, and as a consequence now know everything there is to know, on the subject of the film version of *Dr. Dolittle,* and I am beginning to have my doubts about whether I chose my specialism wisely. (I'm talking here, of course, about the 1967 version starring Rex Harrison, not the later Eddie Murphy vehicle. I don't know anything about that one. I'm not daft.)

This peculiar interest happened by accident, rather than by design. I read Mark Harris's book *Pictures At a Revolution,* which is about the five movies nominated for the 1967 Best Picture Oscar, and Harris's book led me to John Gregory Dunne's *The Studio,* first published in 1969. Inexplicably, *Dr. Dolittle* was, in the opinion of the Academy, one of the five best films—along with *The Graduate, Bonnie and Clyde, In The Heat of the Night,* and *Guess Who's Coming to Dinner*—of 1967. (I say "inexplicably" because I'm presuming the film was tosh—although this presumption is in itself inexplicable, because when I saw it, in 1967, I thought it was a work of rare genius); in *The Studio,* a piece of behind-the-scenes reportage, Dunne was given complete access to the boardrooms and sets of Twentieth Century Fox, a studio that happened to be in the middle of making *Dr Dolittle* at the time.

Fortunately, *Dr. Dolittle* is worth studying, to degree level and possibly beyond. Did you know, for example, that in today's money it cost one hundred and ninety million dollars to make? That Haile Selasse visited the set in L.A., and Rex Harrison asked him, "How do you like *our* jungle?" That the script required a chimpanzee to learn how to cook bacon and eggs in a frying pan, a skill that took Chee-Chee—and his three under-studies—six months to acquire? (I'm pretty sure I picked it up in less than half that time, so all those stories about the intelligence of apes are way wide of the mark.) Some of these stories should be engraved on a plaque and placed outside Grauman's Chinese Theatre in Hollywood, as a monument to the stupidity, vanity, and pointlessness of commercial movie-making.

Pictures of a Revolution is one of the best books about film I have ever read, and if you're remotely interested in the process of making movies—in the process of making anything at all—then you should read it. Of course film-making has an enormous advantage when it comes to insider accounts, because every movie could have taken a different path, had crucial elements not fallen into place at crucial times. Robert Redford wanted to star in *The Graduate;* the writers of *Bonnie and Clyde* were desperate for Truffaut to direct their script, and Warren Beatty, one of the producers, saw Bob Dylan and Shirley Maclaine as the leads. (If only literature could be this interesting. You know, "John Updike was scheduled to write *Catch-22* until right at the last moment. He pulled out when he was unexpectedly offered the first of the Rabbit books, after Saul Bellow's agent couldn't get the deal he wanted for his client...." As usual, books get stiffed with all the dull stories: "He thought up the idea. Then he wrote it. Then it got published." Who wants to read about that?) But Harris certainly exploits this advantage for all it's worth, and he does it with enormous intelligence, sympathy and verve. He builds his compelling plotlines through painstaking accumulation of minute detail, but never lets the detail cloud his sense of momentum, and the end result is a book that you might find yourself unable to put down.

Like the best of those nonfiction books that take a moment in time and shake it until it reveals its resonance, *Pictures of a Revolution* turns out to be about a lot of things. The subtitle indicates one of Harris's theses—that 1967 was a pivotal year in cinema history, the year that the old studio system started to collapse, to be replaced by an independent producer-led culture which still thrives today, although not all of these producers are making *The Graduate* or *Bonnie and Clyde*. Sidney Poitier's emergence as a star with real box-office clout allows Harris to weave the subject of race into his narrative. Poitier starred in two of these five movies, and only just avoided having to appear in *Dr. Dolittle,* too, and he ended up being attacked for letting the side down—the bland liberal pieties of *Guess Who's Coming To Dinner* were deemed particularly offensive—while living in fear of his life whenever he ventured below the Mason-Dixon line. Meanwhile, the influx of saucy European movies that had hip Americans flocking to the cinemas had put ruinous strain on the curious, church-controlled U.S. censorship system, and Harris has fun with all the illogicalities and incongruities that were being backlit by the freedom of the '60s: a bare breast was tolerable in *The Pawnbroker* because it was a movie about the Holocaust, but the naked girls in Antonioni's *Blow-Up* were unacceptable. Harris even finds room for the slow death of one form of movie criticism, as exemplified by the stuffy Bosley Crowther of the *New York Times,* and the sharper, fresher style that Pauline Kael introduced.

Pictures at a Revolution is smart, then, and it feels real, but these qualities are not what make it such an absorbing read—not for me, anyway. I should perhaps admit at this point that for the last four years or so I have been working on a film script, a labor of love that, like all such projects, occasionally looked as though it was unloved by anybody but me. To cut a long, boring, occasionally maddening and frequently depressing story short, it's now being made into a film, as we speak, and I'm sure that the sudden metamorphosis of script into movie made me relish this book even more than I might otherwise have done: on top of all its other virtues, *Pictures at a Revolution* captures perfectly the long, meandering, dirty, and bewildering path from inspiration to production. There's no guarantee, of course, that anyone will ever see this film I've been involved in, but the great thing about Harris's book is that it has 20/20 hindsight, and it makes you feel as if anything might be possible. Who knew that the unemployable twenty-nine-year old actor that Mike Nichols perversely cast in *The Graduate* would turn into Dustin Hoffman? Who could have predicted that the difficult young actress nicknamed, cruelly, "Done Fadeaway" by Steve McQueen would turn out to be the Oscar-winning star of *Network*? In other words, this book creates the illusion of shape and destiny, always useful when you have no sense of either.

As an added bonus, Harris introduced me to a novel that turned out to be a neglected minor classic. Immediately before

Anne Bancroft took the part of Mrs. Robinson in *The Graduate,* she appeared in a small and apparently highly regarded British film called *The Pumpkin Eater,* adapted by Harold Pinter from a 1962 novel by Penelope Mortimer. It's a strange, fresh, gripping book, the story of a woman with five children by three different husbands, now married to a fourth, a successful scriptwriter called Jake Armitage who is sleeping around. If the set-up stretches credulity, it should be pointed out that the plot is scrupulously, dizzyingly autobiographical. Or at least, Penelope Mortimer had a lot of children by several different men—not all of whom she was married to—before marrying the successful English novelist, playwright, scriptwriter and lawyer John Mortimer. One of the many achievements of *The Pumpkin Eater* is that it somehow manages to find the universal truths in what was hardly an archetypal situation: Mortimer peels several layers of skin off the subjects of motherhood, marriage, and monogamy, so that what we're asked to look at is frequently red-raw and painful without being remotely self-dramatizing. In fact, there's a dreaminess to some of the prose that is particularly impressive, considering the tumult that the book describes and, presumably, was written in. Penelope Mortimer's books are mostly out of print, although the wonderful people at Persephone, a publisher that specialises in forgotten twentieth-century novels by women (*Miss Pettigrew Lives For a Day* is one of their notable successes in the UK), are bringing back a couple of them this year.

I'm sorry this section is so gossipy, but *The Pumpkin Eater* sheds an extraordinary light on a story that fascinated both the broadsheets and the tabloids in the UK a while back. In 2004 Sir John Mortimer, as he is now, was apparently surprised but delighted to learn that he had fathered a child with the well-known and much-loved British actress Wendy Craig at the beginning of the 1960s, while married to Penelope; father and son met for the first time in 2004, and have since formed a bond. (Imagine, I don't know, Garrison Keillor owning up to a child conceived with Shirley Jones of the Partridge Family and you will get a sense of the media interest in the story.) And yet in *The Pumpkin Eater,* Jake Armitage impregnates a young actress, just as his wife is being sterilized—a detail that sounds implausibly and melodramatically novelistic, but which is also, according to *A Voyage Round John Mortimer,* Valerie Grove's recently published biography, drawn from life. It is difficult to understand how his illegitimate son could have been a complete surprise to him, given that his wife had written about it in a novel forty-two years before he is supposed to have found out. If Sir John's surprise is genuine, then he is guilty of a far greater crime than infidelity: he never read his wife's stuff. This is unforgivable, and, I would have thought, extremely good grounds for divorce. If I ever caught my wife not reading something I'd written, there'd be trouble.

I have read other things these last few weeks—Graham McCann's intelligent biography of Cary Grant; the great Richard Price's new novel *Lush Life,* which is typically absorbing, real, and breathtakingly plotted; Thurston Clarke's inspiring book about RFK's drive for the Democratic nomination in '68, *The Last Campaign.* But I'm not going to write about them, because this is my last column in *The Believer,* at least for a while, and I wanted to leave some space to bang on about how much I've enjoyed the last five years. In 2003, when I began "Stuff I've Been Reading," I hadn't read *David Copperfield* or Edmund Gosse's *Father and Son.* I'd never read a word by Marilynne Robinson, and *Gilead* hadn't been published. I hadn't read Dylan's *Chronicles, Citizen Vince, The Dirt, How To Breathe Underwater, Hangover Square, Feed, Skellig....* (And, on a more mournful note, two of my favourite contemporary writers, Lorrie Moore and Elizabeth McCracken, have managed to avoid being included in the "Books Read" list through the simple but devious method of not writing anything since the column began.) I have been reading great books since I was sixteen or so, which means that I should have described one-seventh of my most memorable reading experiences in these pages, but it really feels like more than that: you, dear reader, have helped me to choose more wisely than I might otherwise have done, and to read a little bit more vigorously. And quitting (because, despite all the fistfights and legal problems I've had with the Polysyllabic Spree, they never did have the guts to fire me) worries me, because there must be a chance that I'll sink back into my old reading habits: until 2003, I lived exclusively on a diet of chick-lit novels, Arsenal programs from the 1970s, and my own books. At the moment, though, I am telling myself that I'm leaving because I want to read lots of Victorian novels that you wouldn't want to read about, a lie that lets me walk out with dignity, and hope for the future. Thank you for listening, those of you that did—I'll miss you all. ✷

Nick Hornby is the author of the novels *A Long Way Down*, *How to Be Good*, *High Fidelity*, and *About a Boy*, as well as *Slam*, a novel for young adults. He also wrote a memoir, *Fever Pitch*, as well as *Songbook*, which was a finalist for a National Book Critics Circle Award. His two previous collections of writing from the *Believer* magazine are *The Polysyllabic Spree* and *Housekeeping vs. the Dirt*.

NICK
HORNBY
HAS STOPPED
READING

It's true: the September 2008 column that ends this book was Hornby's last column for the magazine. But the magazine, blasted and saddened to lose such a reliable source of humor and intelligence, itself remains a reliable source of humor and intelligence: the legendary critic Greil Marcus has a monthly column; we count Zadie Smith, Jim Shepard, and Rick Moody among our regular contributors; and three annual special issues come with excellent bonus items, such as the crazily popular music issue's CD compilation. Just fill out the form below for a special Hornbyphile discount!

or subscribe for no discount at all at **believermag.com/subscribe**

. . . .